BELLY DANCE RHYTHM RESOURCE

What Every Dancer Should Know for a Memorable Performance

by

Richard Adrian Steiger, M.A.

Anaphase Publishing
A DIVISION & IMPRINT OF CYBERLEPSY MEDIA

**Belly Dance
Rhythm Resource**

What Every Dancer
Should Know
for a
Memorable Performance
revised edition

Most chapters of this book have been revised and reprinted from
The Papyrus, the official publication of
SAMEDA (San Diego Area Middle-Eastern Dance Association)
from 2007–2013, in both print and Web versions

"The Shapes of Sound: The Dumbek Drum Family" was reprinted from
The Belly Dance Reader 2, published by Gilded Serpent, 2014, pp 174–78
ISBN 13: 978–0-692248-33-1

Maps by Free Vector Maps, at HTTP://FREEVECTORMAPS.COM

ISBN 10: 0-945962-50-9
ISBN 13: 978-0-945962-50-2

Published and Printed in the United States of America

by

Anaphase Publishing
A DIVISION & IMPRINT OF CYBERLEPSY MEDIA

Table of Contents

Preface

"Belly" dance is an ancient art-form born of mysticism and ritual, evolved through the centuries to entertain and enthrall. The music of *Le Danse Orientale* is no less enchanting, transcending its ancient roots to encompass rhythms from not only the Near- and Middle-East, but Africa, Persia, India, and even Latin America.

Richard Adrian Steiger draws upon his extensive education in ethnomusicology to bring dancers into the rich world of belly dance music, in all its permutations. His exquisite sensitivity to the nuances of ethnic rhythms transcends ordinary understanding. In short, tightly-focused chapters, he is able to inform and inspire beginning and seasoned dancers alike.

Let this work guide you through the multi-rhythmic world of belly dance music, enhance your training with expert advice and encouragement, and transform your performances into memorable events.

—*Lily Splane (aka, "Layla" in another life)*
November, 2014

Belly Dance Rhythm Resource

SECTION I

MUSIC FUNDAMENTALS

Belly Dance Music Enjoys World-Wide Influences

(shaded areas indicate countries with musical influence)

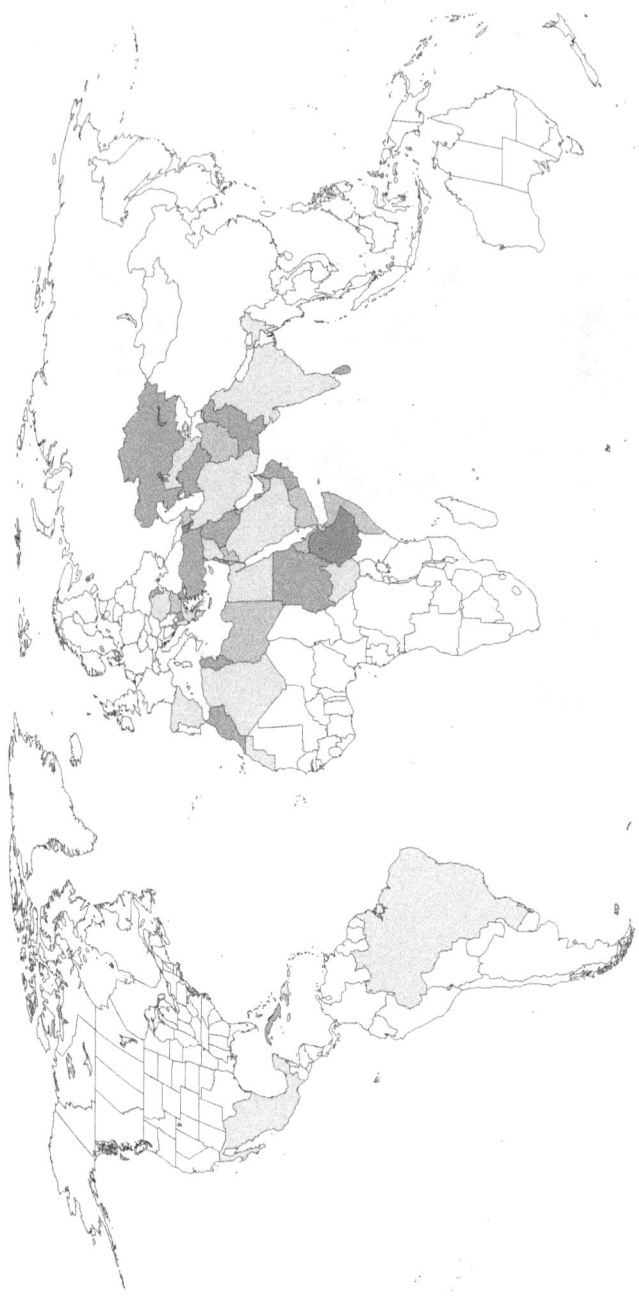

INTRODUCTION

In the same way a musician who accompanies belly dance should be educated about the basics of movement and form, a dancer should know the names and structures of the rhythms to which she dances. It is the intent of these chapters to familiarize dancers with these rhythms, and to help dancers develop rhythmic skills.

Rhythmic patterns used by the modern belly dance community in the United States are derived from many sources. Principle among them are those of the Arabs and Turks. In addition, Persian, Greek, Armenian, Balkan, various African sources, Central Asian, and Western rhythms infuse the selections available to the dancer. As belly dance evolves, alternative rhythms become more and more present in performance.

This book seeks first—in Section I—to establish a strong foundation of musical basics, upon which may be built proficiency with the principle traditional rhythms of modern belly dance. *Masmudi, Baladi, Maqsum, Fellâhi, Sa'idi, Ayyub, Chiftetelli, Karshlamá,* and other standard *danse orientale* rhythms, should not be a mystery. Each chapter of Sections II and III of this book will feature a separate rhythm, including its origin, name, and context. Section IV will further explore specific folk and ethnic rhythms often integrated into modern belly dance, such as the *Boléro, Bandari, Chobiyyah,* and *Debke.*

Belly dance rhythms can therefore be recognized by ear as simple repeating melodies constructed of primary drum-notes. The educated dancer needs to be able to—like the musician— instantly recognize and reproduce the basic pattern of the common rhythms, and ultimately to express coherent movement that transcends the mundane.

Drummers use the drum-note melody as an always-present, iterative foundation upon which to elaborate, ornament, and to interact with the dancer. Dancers use the rhythm to guide the form of their movements. The elaborations and ornamentations are a dialog between drummer and dancer. The link between rhythm and motion is the heart of dance. The drummer brings time alive, and dancers bring motion to space.

—Richard Adrian Steiger
November, 2014

CHAPTER 1: THE BASICS

Three Musical Essentials for Dancers

How often have I heard, "I don't care about music theory, I just want to dance." Well, ok, it is good to be spontaneous, but... the more you understand your art on a theoretical level, the deeper the layers of expression become. General music theory is the contemplation and understanding of the fundamentals or rudiments of music (its sound and structure). The following three musical essentials will take you far. It is a lifetime learning adventure. Keep the passion and expression, but base that on applied knowledge.

1. The Fundamentals of Rhythm

The basis of music with a "beat" is simple. Upon these elements complexity can arise.

- Pulse (primary points; the matrix)
- Beat and subdivision (down- and up-beats)
- Cycle (the frame in which rhythms are set)

Beats are subdivided by pulses. Cycles of beats create the frame in which rhythms (accented and unaccented, short and long durations of sounds—like poetry) exist.

2. The Basic Belly Dance Rhythms

Belly dance rhythms are composed of low- (*dum*) and high-pitched (*tek*) drum-note sequences—kind of a simple melody. Although there are many rhythms, you should be able to recognize the standard ones in the list below from recordings

or in a live setting. Ideally, you should be able to finger-count the cycle while reciting the rhythm. At the least, you should be able to clap the beat and recite the rhythm. You need to become familiar with these standard rhythms and how they are danced:

- The *masmudi* family—*masmudi* (eight-beat cycle), *baladi* (four-beat cycle), *maqsum* (four-beat cycle), *fellâhi* (two-beat cycle), *sai'di* (four-beat cycle)
- *Ayyub* (two-beat cycle)
- *Chiftetelli* (eight-beat cycle)
- *Karshlamá* [Greek—*karsilamas*] (nine-beat cycle)

Take the time to be an active listener to music. What is the rhythm and its cycle? Can you clap your hands on the beat and keep up with the tempo changes? How does the tempo affect the feel? For example, *baladi* is not *sa'idi*—the dance moves for each are different.

3. Forms and Structures: Suites and Solos

When it comes to forms and structures, there are many. Arabic and Turkish belly dance routines are set in a suite form. In other words, there are several parts (three to seven) strung together, each piece with a different rhythm. A typical medium-length suite for belly dance begins with a fast entry section (e.g., *ayyub* or *fellâhi*) which merges into the first medium tempo piece (e.g., *baladi* or *maqsum*). The music slows down into a sensuous piece (e.g., *chiftetelli* or *masmudi*) in which the dancer does veil or "floor work." At the conclusion, the drummer stands out and begins the drum solo (freestyle). When complete, the music then shifts in to an up-tempo piece or two (back to *baladi* or *sa'idi*, or even *karshlamá*) in which the dancer "works" the room. The suite may end with a repeat of the entry music (e.g., *ayyub* or *fellâhi*), except that it is instead, for exiting. These parts can

be assembled, and added to or subtracted from, in any way the dancer and musicians agree. The recognition of the rhythms is critical to how the dancer moves. Each rhythm has its own characteristic for the dancer to express. Variety counts.

The drum solo (a section in a suite) has a loose form that is quite variable. This is the section where the dancer and drummer (as artists) can be playful and passionate, allowing each other to shine. Typically, the solo starts with a continuation of the rhythm from the preceding piece of music in the suite. The rhythm intensifies and begins to morph into accented patterns. These patterns are repeated, so that the dancer can have time to identify and respond to them. After a while, depending upon signals from the dancer, the drummer shifts to rapid continuous rolling patterns with accents in the part known to dancers as the "shimmy." These parts in the solo can shift from loud to soft and fast to slow and back. When the dancer signals she's had enough, the drummer ends the solo with a flourish—the duo hitting that final beat together. Although there are stock riffs (like in ice dancing), in a sense, this is improvisational jazz at its best— within reason (or not), anything goes. Expect the unexpected. The dancer's knowledge of the fundamentals of rhythm are essential to her ability to recognize and synchronize to what the drummer is playing. Relax and have fun.

Final Thoughts

Keep an open mind. Try not to shut down when the word "theory" is mentioned. It is all about applying primary knowledge. It is true that people could go through life not knowing how to read or write, but...what a greater world it is when they can! Spend time learning the rhythmic fundamentals. Incorporate them into your practice. Realize them in your performance.

CHAPTER 2: THE SHAPES OF THE DUMBEK FAMILY

This chapter seeks to define the four basic shapes of the *dumbek* (pronounced "DOOM-bek") drum family—a percussive instrument group used for music throughout northern Africa, the Middle- and Near-East (Levant), and Balkan, Greek, Turkish, and Persian countries. The dumbek (also known as the *dumbeg, darbuka, derbeki, tabla arabi, deblek, tombak,* and *zerbaghali,* among other names, spellings, and pronunciations) is classified in western musicology as a single-headed, open-ended, goblet- or chalice-shaped *membranophone.* Its primary sound generator, the drumhead, is an elastic membrane made of skin or plastic stretched over the mouth of the drum body. Local culture, custom, and availability of materials determine the preferences of sound, size, shape, and material from which the drum is made.

The Drum

The drums of the dumbek family are physically characterized by an upper resonator chamber fused to a lower tube. The waist diameter between the resonator chamber and the effusor governs the passage of the air flow out of the tube into the performance space. This is relevant because the smaller the waist, the less air passes from the resonator chamber into the tube and out of the drum when the drumhead is struck. The result of this ratio effects the sounding time of the fundamental pitch. The fundamental is the low-pitched open tone produced by the whole drumhead when it is struck in its central area. Think of a stone thrown to the center of a circular pool, and concentric rippling back and forth between the center and edge until it fades away to its steady state. On the dumbek *(et al),* this low tone is called "dum"

(Arabic, Turkish or Farsi: "tom"). A wide-waisted drum's less enclosed chamber effuses the soundwaves into the atmosphere quickly, damping the drumhead vibrations. The small-waisted drumhead's vibrations are prolonged by regeneration due to the enclosed chamber and small outlet for the air.

The physical environment in which the instrument is played has an effect upon its resonance. Sound can be reflected off of a surface or absorbed by it. Small-waisted drums are self-contained resonators due to their form, but are enhanced by resonant rooms. Wide-waisted drums are more effected by the space in which they are used. In a non-reflective space such as outdoors (although buildings can reflect) or in a carpeted room with people and furniture, they produce sounds of a short duration. The "dum" is not prolonged. The same drum played in an enclosed space with reflective surfaces (mirrors, tiles, hardwood floors, hard surface walls, etc.) will sound longer. It will sound "bigger" than it is. The reason is that the drum acoustically interfaces with the atmosphere around it, extending its native acoustic properties. Performance in reflective spaces is an important physical context for traditional music through all the regions the dumbek family is found.

Drum shells are made from various materials ranging from clay (earthenware, stoneware, white porcelain), hard and soft woods (ash, mulberry, walnut, tangerine/lemon fruit-woods, cedar, pine), and metals (aluminum, copper, brass). Although they have an effect on whether the drumhead vibrations are absorbed or reflected within the resonance chamber, the flexibility (softness) or stiffness (hardness) of material has little to do with the drum's resonance. The principle contribution the material makes is to the timbre of the high-pitched drum stroke called *tek* (or *taak*). Made at the edge of the drum on its rim, *tek* is the opposite drum-

tone of the low-pitched *dum*. This drum-tone is a sonic mixture of both the drum head's native sound and the characteristic sound of the material of the shell: like a bell (metallic), a block of wood (woody), or a hollow clay vessel (ceramic).

The drum head (organic or synthetic) has the most effect on the subjective quality of "musicalness" of the sound of the instrument, as it is the primary vibrator: the sound maker. Organic drumheads are considered "warmer" sounding than "cold" plastic. However, modern formulations made by companies like Remo, have come up with synthetic emulations of animal skin that are quiet satisfactory and have comparable tone. They also don't require the use of heat to be tuned. The plastic also rejects all water absorption.

Like any musical instrument, the sound of the dumbek is the sum of its parts: the type, quality, and tension of the drumhead, the shape and volume of the resonator chamber, the waist, the tube, and its acoustic context.

The Shapes

Based upon resonator shape, the four principle types of drums of the dumbek family are:

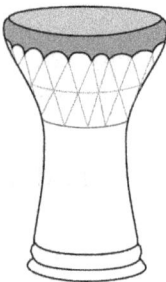 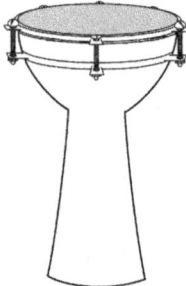 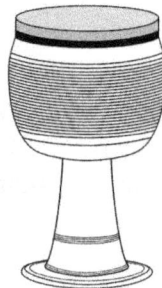 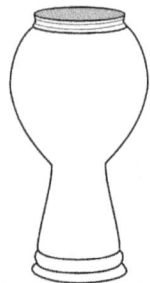

1: Cone　　*2: Hemisphere*　　*3: Cylinder*　　*4: Globe*

Cone

The conical resonator is associated with Arabic speaking people, and with the regions of Egypt, Lebanon, Libya, and Saudi Arabia. It is not limited to these areas. In tandem with the hemispherical resonator dumbek (see below), the conical form is the most well-known shape in Europe and the United States. Based upon the *fellahîn* drum (*hoqa* and *fekhar*) developed along the Nile Delta, the conical resonator type is most identified with Egypt.

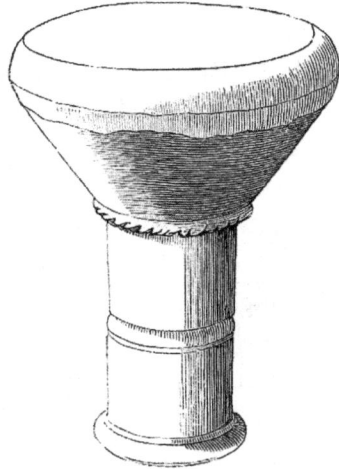

*The Wilkinson "Darabooka,"
a fellahîn-style drum*

The resonator is attached at a wide waist to a straight or concave tube, with some variation. The oldest forms have straight tubes. The example above was collected around 1850.

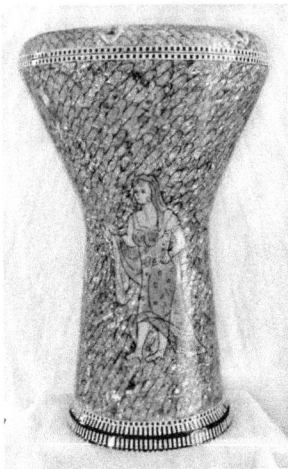

Aluminum tabla arabi

Breakage of clay drums, and the effects of weather on drumheads, have made the modern cast aluminum and plastic *tabla arabi* the dominant drum type in the modern Arab musical markets of the world. This kind of sand-cast drum is sometimes known as the "Alexandria" drum—an eponymous term that came about through a uniform agreement that these types of drums were first produced in the Egyptian port on the western edge of the Nile Delta in Egypt.

Hemisphere

The hemispherical resonator dumbek is characterized by a bowl attached at a small waist to a straight, convex, concave, or conical tube. It is made of either clay, sheet metal (brass or copper), or extruded from aluminum. The sheet metal hemispherical resonator drum is thought to have originated in the metalworking industries of Damascus in Syria. Metal extrusion to make drums is thought to have developed in Turkey after WWII. Armenian and Turkish musicians popularized this kind of drum in the U.S. before the Arabic-associated conical drum *(tabla arabi)* became popular beginning in the late 1970s. The term *dumbeg* (Armenian, note the "g") became synonymous with the instrument. Through changes in dialect and translation, the "g" became a "k," hence the current spelling as "dumbek" (note the "k").

Turkish clay dumbek

Turkish metal dumbek

Cylinder

Cylindrical resonator "chalice"-type drums, exemplified by the one called the *tombak*, seem to be particular to the Persian culture and the Iranian region. Its sound is characterized the prolongation of the low drum-tone, *tom,* caused by the large size of the resonator and the small waist. The Persian tombak is made of lathe-turned wood with either straight or curved sides, and a footed-base at the bottom of the tube. Traditional surface finishes leave the drum natural or set with mosaic design. The addition of a ribbed surface is dated to the 1960s and attributed to the influence of tombak virtuoso Ostad Tehrani (1912–1974). Relief carving has gained recent popularity.

Straight tombak   *Khatam tombak*   *Carved tombak*

Globe

The globular resonator form is old. It is also rare outside of the north-western region of coastal Africa where it is found. The distinct globular shape of the resonator may be a thread of ancient Mediterranean ceramic work—perhaps based upon inverted wine and oil containers.

Made of clay, the globe shape of the upper section takes on a variety of curves: rounded, squashed, and elongated. Most globe-type drums have some kind of variation of a curved rim flange used to attach the drumhead.

The globular form may be divided into two groups:

1. A resonator distinct from the tube at the waist

Globe drum 1 *Globe drum 2*

2. A resonator and tube merged into a vase

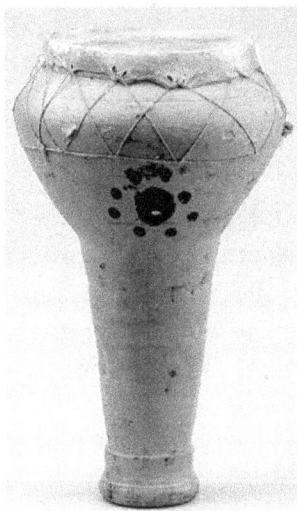

Vase-type globe drum

Regionality

The following list presents a tentative set of general preferences for dumbek types based upon geographical region. Although drums are bonded to region and culture, the mixing and borrowing of instruments and musical ideas from around the world, through present-day telecommunication, has changed the traditional associations.

Northern Preferences

The hemispherical-shaped bowl resonator is associated with Balkan, Greek, Turkish, Armenian and Syrian regions. The drum is called the *toumbeleki* (Greek) or the *dumbek,* or *deblek*

(Turkey). Regional and local name variants specific or associated with this type of drum also include *darbuka* and *derbeki* (Greek-Turkish-Syrian). (Picken, 215–33; Anoyankis, 1234–6)

Southern Preferences

The conical-shaped bowl resonator is associated with Arab speaking culture, and Egyptian *fellahîn*. The terms *hoqa* and *fehker* (Arabic, "clay") are used for the rural river mud terracotta drum made in the Nile Delta and along the river. The modernized aluminum version of the drum, also made in Egypt, is called the *tabl* or *tabla (arabi)*. The mass influx of this drum into the U.S., Europe, and around the world has popularized it. The terms *dumbek* and *tabla* are now being used concurrently. It depends on the company you are with as to what to call the drum; region and custom prevail in traditional settings. (Wilkinson, 143; Hickmann, 228–245)

Northeastern Preferences

The cylindrical-shaped bowl resonator drum called the *tombak* is associated with Persian culture and in general with Iran. There are variants of it, notably the clay *zerbaghali* (Pashtun, "under the arm,") from Afghanistan. The tombak first appeared in historical imagery during the Qajar Period (1787–1925). (Zonis, 173; and Bida painting, 1850) Its roots are far older. (Nashepour, 2001)

Maghreb Preferences

The globular-shaped bowl resonator is associated with north-western Africa: Morocco, Algeria, Tunisia, Libya, where it is called the *darbuka*. An example of the rare vase-type globular drum, the *stamna*, is found in the eastern Aegean islands of

Lesbos and Chios, and on Crete. (Anoyanakis, 134–6; Collaer and Elsner, 78)

Conclusion

A group of morphologically related drums is not far fetched. The dumbek family of drums, as herein described, have both a common form (a resonator attached to a tube) and geographical relationship (the Mediterranean). For reasons yet unknown, at least four distinct divisions of preference for shape (and presumably sound) are associated with both geography and culture:

1. Arabic speaking people: *cone*
2. Greek, Turkish, Armenian, Syrian: *hemisphere*
3. Persian culture/Iran: *cylinder*
4. Northwestern Africa and Aegean region: *globe, vase*

CHAPTER 3: TABLA OR *TABLAS*?

There is confusion over the term *tabla* within the belly dance world. *Tabla* means different things (drums) to different cultures. It is a simple error, based upon the root word for drum, *tbl*. This chapter aims to clarify the origin and use of the word in the Arabic-speaking Middle East, and in the Hindi- and Dravidian-speaking Indian subcontinent.

The word *tabla*, among Egyptian-Arabic musicians, is used to refer to a specific conical-type clay drum (the "Egyptian," "Arabic," or "Nile" drum, depending upon the variation in the shape of the resonator tube on the drum. (SEE ILLUSTRATION) It is different from the bowl-type northern drum associated with Turkey, Syria, and Armenia called the *dumbek* (a term derived from the sounds of the drum). The same words are used for the same types of drums, making it even more confusing. The term *tabl* (Arabic), meaning drum, is thought to have its ancient roots in the Aramaic term *tabla*, and the Akkadian word *tabalu* or *tapalu*. T(a)bl is used as a prefix in conjunction with names of Arabic drums, such as *tabl al-baladi*. The drum called the *tabl al-baladi* is a double-headed wooden instrument played with sticks and hands, often in Sa'idi music. *Tabla* is pronounced, in Arabic, with a reduction of the first vowel, and with emphasized consonants, to sound more like *TBLah*. A version of the Nile drum called the *toumbaknari* is found in coastal Pakistan and in Kashmir. The name derives from *tumbak* and *nari* (clay pot). The original form of the drum was probably brought there by Arabic sailors.

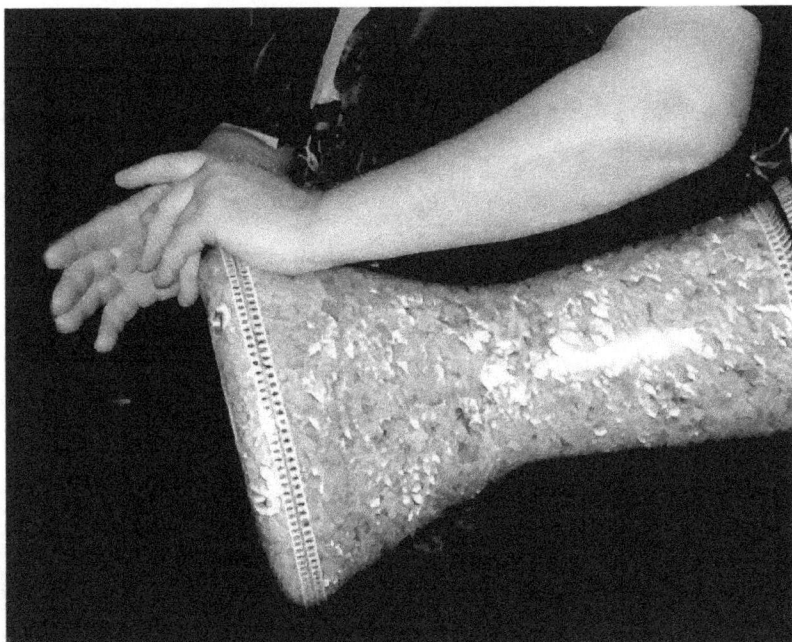

The Egyptian-Arabic conical-type tabla (dumbek)

The use of the word *tabla* to refer to the Egyptian-style drum began around the late 1950s among club musicians in the Levant (samri) and main Arabic centers (masri) such as Cairo and Alexandria. What was previously called the *derbeki* or *darabukka* (a generic term used for the dumbek throughout the Mediterranean), became the tabla. One may speculate that this was the result of choosing the Arabic tabla over the classical Arabic mosaic tambourine called the riq ("rick," Arabic). In the context of amplified stage music, the Arabic tabla and Turkish-Syrian-Armenian dumbek became the rhythmically versatile drum that dominated the rhythmic aspects of the music. In current times, the Arabic *tabla* is played as a solo instrument (i.e., the only instrument to accompany a dancer where no other

melody instrument is used—drum solo), in addition to fulfilling a role as a rhythmic accompaniment in music groups.

The term *tablas* (with an "s" added) means (to people in the North and South Indian cultures, and among the Afghani, Pakistani, and other areas connected to India) a paired drum array. (SEE ILLUSTRATION, BELOW) The Indian and Arabic words share the same word root—*tabl*.

North Indian tablas
(tabla, daya, or dhaina, right hand; and baya or duggi, left hand)

The *tabla* drums are specific to North India, and are considered derived from earlier barrel drums (cut in half to form a pair). The *tablas* are associated with classical music and rhythmic theory (*tala*), although they are used in urban and folk music as well. The tablas (*baya(n)* or *duggi*, left; and *tabla*, *daya(n)*, or

dhaina, right) have distinctive physical features on their multi-layered playing heads. The black spots (laminated to the center of the right-hand drum, and offset on the left-hand drum) are variously called *shyahi* (*siahi*, *gub*, or *ak*), from the Farsi word for black, *siah*. The black spot functions as a nodal damper allowing for melodic playing. The melodic sound of the *tablas* is realized by where and how the hand and fingers strike the surface of these complex drumheads. The *tablas* have not been a solo instrument in the same way as the Arabic *tabla* (*dumbek*, *darabuka*, etc.), until recently. Indian tablas more often are paired with the sitar, flute, or voice, and played in ensembles.

The word *tabla* is most well known, on a world-wide level, to mean the Indian drums. The current practice of calling the Middle Eastern bowl-type drum a tabla (more commonly known as the *dumbek*, *darbuka*, *derbecki*, *toumbeleki*, or *deblek*) is gaining popularity in the West, mostly promoted by Arabic-speaking musicians.

North Indian tablas
(tabla, daya, or dhaina, right hand; and baya or duggi, left hand)

CHAPTER 4: FIVE FRAMES

Frame drums have been used since very ancient times, long before any other configuration of membrane and shell. In belly dance music, although the *dumbek* (*tabla*, etc.) is the current drum of choice, frame drums provide an alternative sound and style. The following is a small sample of some of the current instruments that the author has used as the sole drum for an accompaniment.

Standard Riq

The first example is a *riq*. The *riq* (pronounced somewhere between *reek*, *rick*, or *ruhk* depending upon the region) is the traditional keeper of the rhythmic mode in Arabic classical music—the *tabla arabi* (dumbek) only gaining ascendancy to this role early in the last century. The *riq* is always present in drum *takhts* (see "Chapter 45: The Drum Takht" in Section V). The characteristic part of the *riq* is the five sets of dual cymbals set around the shell. They allow an extra dimension of expressivity. Although it's volume of sound is somewhat quiet in a modern electric setting, a microphone can solve that problem. The example shown on the next page has a calfskin head rather than the traditional fish-skin. Because it is an organic head (and this is true for all drums with these kinds of drumheads), it is susceptible to the intake of moisture in the skin cells which lowers the pitch of the head—it relaxes the head tension when humidified. A heating pad is used to temper the head (driving the moisture out). This can be frustrating, and may require having two instruments (one on the heater and the other in use) that the player exchanges when the pitch lowers too much.

Riq Measurements

DIMENSION	MEASUREMENT
Outside	8.50"±
Inside	7.75"±
Depth	2.25"±
Shell	0.75"

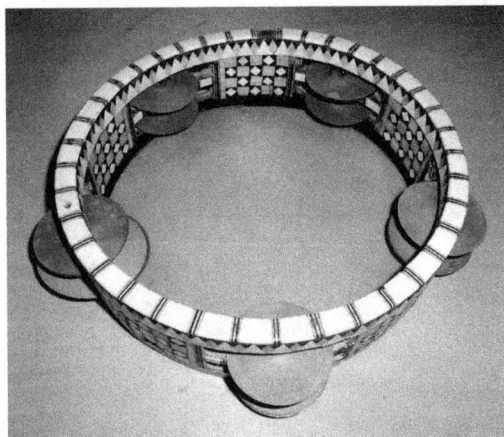

Riq with natural skin head, underside

Riq with natural skin head, top surface

Tunable Riq

The second example is a modern, tunable *riq*. It is made of composite man-made materials and has mechanical tuners. It is impervious to water and always stays tuned.

Tunable Riq Measurements

DIMENSION	MEASUREMENT
Outside	8.9"±
Inside	8.6"±
Depth	2.4"±
Shell	0.4"

Tunable Riq, top surface

Tunable Riq, underside

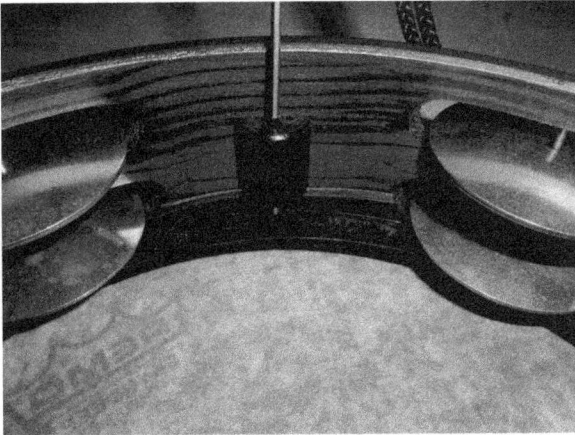

Tunable Riq, close-up of tuning screw with inserted tuning key

Tar

The *tar* is a "jingleless" big-diameter frame-drum associated with the Sudan, but found widely in Arabic music representing the "bedouin" sound. The example shown here is a modern version made of synthetic materials. The tar is a very expressive

instrument, and loud. The *tar* is also an instrument of the drum *takht* (a traditional ensemble of drummers), discussed at length in "Chapter 45: The Drum Takht" in Section V.

Tar Measurements

DIMENSION	MEASUREMENT
Outside	18.00"±
Inside	17.25"±
Depth	3.00"±
Shell	0.25"

Tar, lying face down to expose inside surface

Tar, being held for scale comparison

Daf

The *daf* is a big-diameter frame-drum with ring-jingles, found throughout Iran. It is associated with Kurdish music, and with Sufism. The daf shown below was made in Iran by the Helmi family. The shell is made of wood, but the head is synthetic with no tuning issues. Although not a traditional instrument for belly dance, it is completely capable of such a task.

Daf Measurements

DIMENSION	MEASUREMENT
Outside	20.75"±
Inside	20.00"±
Depth	2.25"±
Shell	0.50"±

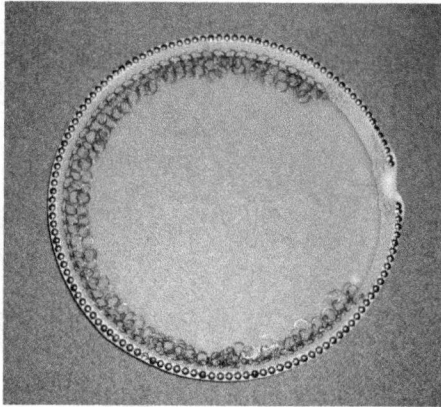

Daf, showing underside with attached metallic "jingles"

Pejman Hadadi playing the daf (Signature Sound Studios, 1998)

Daireh

The *daireh* (DAWH-ee-ray—in Farsi this means "circle") is smaller in diameter than the *daf,* and may or may not have ring-jingles depending on where it was made. In general it is associated with the Caucasus and Azerbaijan, and Iran. It is a "delicate" instrument, but is capable of great power. In other words, its volume range is wide. The example depicted below was made in Iran by the Helmi family.

Daireh Measurements

DIMENSION	MEASUREMENT
Outside	8.50"±
Inside	7.75"±
Depth	2.25"±
Shell	0.75"

Daireh, showing underside with metallic "jingle" rings

Daireh being held to show scale

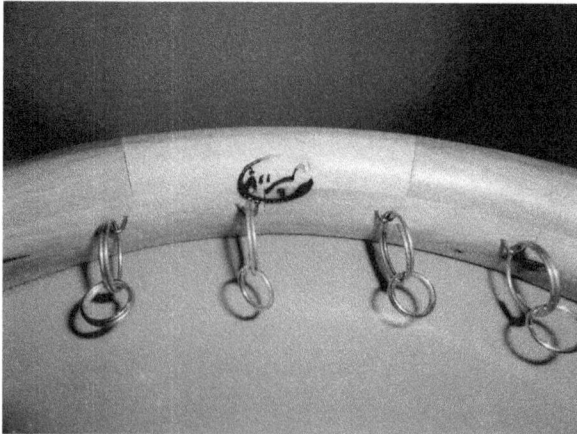

Daireh close-up, showing attached metallic "jingles"

Daireh being held to show scale (note the delicate, thin, translucent playing surface that imparts a clear tone)

Bendir

The *bendir* is a medium diameter frame-drum with snares, found in the Maghreb and in particular through the Atlas Mountain Regions stretching through Morocco and into Algeria and Lybia. The example shown has three snares (thin strings against the drum head that buzz like a snare drum in a drumset). The head on this drum is organic and thin. Because of that, it requires heating to keep it tight. As a desert instrument it's fine, but in a nightclub it is problematic. Nonetheless, under the right conditions, this instrument, like the aforementioned *tar*, is capable of being quite loud and very expressive. The snares give it, like the jingles and cymbal disks in the other frames, an extra expressive dimension (one lacking on the dumbek).

Bendir Measurements

DIMENSION	MEASUREMENT
Outside	14.00"±
Inside	13.50"±
Depth	3.60"±
Shell	0.25"

Bendir, showing underside surface

Bendir, showing top playing surface

As can be seen in this short survey, there are a variety of ways a frame drum can be designed. Each one has its own tradition.

The larger the frame, the more regions for tonal possibilities. Choose your frame-drum carefully, taking your desire for tonal variety into consideration.

Frame drums provide valuable ways for a percussionist to create patterns for belly dancers, without relying upon the same old sound of the dumbek. It should be noted that the rhythms used on the dumbek derive from the older traditions of these frame drums. Keep your eyes and ears open for these drums.

All photos by R.A. Steiger, except those listed in References.

CHAPTER 5: FUNDAMENTAL SKILLS

There are numerous theoretical and practical systems of musical time in different cultures around the world. In traditional classical Arabic, Turkish, and Persian music, poetic scansion and geometrical devices are used to create rhythmic structure. A line of poetry (with its segments and arrangements of short and long syllables/words) can both define the length of time, and identify a specific rhythm—a *rhythmic mode*. Circles (the shape implying a cycle) can be divided. However, unless strictly observing the classical methodology of these cultures for traditional performance, modern practice reduces the "rules" to a fundamental and universal constant. Thus musical time is organized into interrelated layers: the *pulse,* the *beat* and its *tempo,* the *cycle,* and the *rhythm.* Any performer interacting with or creating music should understand these basics, and should have the fundamental skills noted in this article.

Pulse

The pulse flow is the bottom layer, the *grid,* upon which beats are set. An easy way to visualize this concept is to look at a piece of grid paper (like the paper that architects or mathematicians use). The empty spaces of the grid boxes are the matrix of the pulses. Now think of those spaces (a line of them stretching to infinity) like the ticking of a clock's second-hand. A *pulse flow* is regular like the ticking seconds of a clock. To repeat, this is the fundamental layer of musical time. It is a neutral measurement with no accents or gaps.

Beat

In musical terms a pulse *is* a beat. But, while they are the same thing on a technical level, they are thought of differently in practice. A hierarchy is used so that a beat is considered to be made of pulses.

To understand the relationship between a pulse and a beat, try this simple exercise. Clap your hands. On the clap, say "one." Now, clap your hands in evenly spaced intervals continuing to say "one." Half-way between each clap, say "and." Repeat this for a while ("one, and," etc.), feeling the downbeat (the "one") and the upbeat (the "and"). You are now *subdividing* a beat into two even pulses (1:2). This is just the beginning, the foundation, of what may be done with musical time. Knowing this simple skill is a powerful key to understanding rhythm.

Tempo

In music, the *rate* (or pace) at which the pulse/beat foundation flows is called the *tempo*. *Tempi* (plural) in Western music theory are referenced to clocks. For practical purposes, tempo indications, e.g., 60 beats per minute (bpm), are based upon the beat (a larger element) rather than the pulses (a smaller element) that subdivide it. Time flow is subjectively described as being some degree of slow, medium, or fast. Sixty bpm is considered slow compared to 120 bpm.

Tempo is directly related to the emotional expression of a performance. Dancers should develop the skill to synchronize to the tempo of the beat and to the underlying pulse. Repeat the exercise described above ("one, and"). While you clap and recite, note the speed at which you are clapping. Reduce the speed until you consider it to be "slow." Keep the downbeat steady. Clap for

longer than a few moments. Sustain this for a period of time. Now change the tempo and bring it up to a "medium" speed, then after a while move up to a "fast" speed. During this experiment, stay focused on the intervals of time between the down- and up-beats. Each window of tempo has its own quality. When melody and rhythm are superimposed upon this foundational structure (pulse and beat) the tempo effects their expression. Try this: Recite some little poetic saying you know well, over and over. Do it at different speeds. This will give you a direct experience in the effect tempo has on sonic expression.

Cycle

Beats are organized into repeating groups called *cycles*. For example, a cycle of 4 means there are four regular beats that repeat. The first beat of a cycle is typically accented in order to define that it is the "one" of the cycle. In western music, a single cycle is called a *measure* or *bar*. A piece of music is made up of a sequence of many measures. Using the clapping/reciting exercise noted above, change the words you say from "one, and," to "one, and, two, and." This is a cycle of two beats. All dance music (and therefore its rhythms) used in belly dance (except non-pulsed sections) is set in a time cycle. There are many cycles used in belly dance music—for example, cycles of two, three, four, five, six, seven, eight, and so on. Clap along with your favorite music. First find the beat. This is the most salient or obvious undercurrent in the music to which everything synchronizes. Next see if you can, while clapping along, perceive the pulses of subdivision. Once you are locked into the beat, start counting. Can you determine the beginning of the cycle? Clue: Melodies often start on it, and repeated rhythmic patterns played on drums more often than not clearly define the "one" downbeat.

Rhythm

Rhythms are patterns made of durations of sound or silence. An easy way to understand this is to think of the short and long syllables that make up the words of poetry. Clap your hands in an even beat and recite a limerick. Limericks are defined forms with an internal structure (like music), and may easily be recited while clapping. The words of the limerick are rhythmical patterns set over a fundamental grid of pulse, beat, and cycle, unfolding at the tempo you choose to make the words expressive in the way you wish.

The next time you listen to your favorite music, belly dance or otherwise, think of the fundamental pulse, beat, tempo, and cycle. Clap your hands with the music and try to hear where the beat is. How is it subdivided into a pulse flow, what kind of cycle is used, and how does the rhythm interact with the underlying structure of musical time? Once you have these skills, it will be easier to dance to any music, and it will help you recognize and interact with belly dance rhythms.

_____

Author's Note: If you teach dance classes, bring in a musician who can teach these fundamental skills and rhythm recognition to your students.

CHAPTER 6: THE BEAT AND ITS DIVISIONS

For dancers, learning the core of musical time—how to keep the beat—is as important as breathing. A beat in music is an accented mark along a regular flow of pulses in time during a music performance. The beat is the principle underlying organizing structure of time in dance music. It is the building block of the creation of cycles and rhythms. Although this Section addresses musical skill as a general issue, recurring experiences have led the author to realize that there is a real need for dancers to understand this specific concept and skill. It is the most basic connection the dancer has to the music.

Concept # 1

Clap your hands a few times:

X   X   X   X   X   X   X   X

Analyze what you just did. If you clapped so that the interval (blank or "empty" space) between each clap was equal, then "you are keeping a beat," as a musician would say it. A beat means the moment of the mark along the flow of time, in this case the clap of the hands. A beat also means the interval of time *between* each clap. A beat is thus a marked interval of time. The length of the interval or duration of time between marks (claps) is dependent on the rate, or tempo, of the beats.

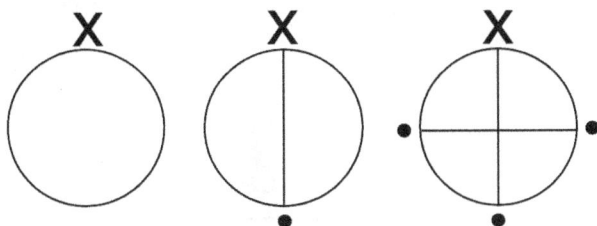

Concept # 2

The whole interval of time between the beats can be divided, or as musicians say, "subdivided," into smaller segments. The reason for this is practical. The visualization of this blank space as a structure (matrix) within which to weave rhythmic patterns, helps the musician keep track of where they are in the time flow. Rhythm exists in a dynamic relationship with the current of time and the space between the beats.

The simplest subdivision is to divide a single interval of time in half—expressing the primary symmetrical division of a whole.

Clap your hand once and hold. The moment of the clap is called the *down-beat*.

Move your hands away from each other to the half-way point between the claps. This point, the apex, is called the *up-beat*.

The following example notates a beat subdivided in half—showing it as being constructed of two pulses. The standard way among musicians to vocalize these particular pulses is to say "one" for the down-beat (the moment of clap), and "and" for the up-beat (the apex between each clap). The "X" in the notation represents the clap on One. The underline indicates that the beat is divided in half (this is a musical convention in notation).

Clap and recite this a few times; keep the speed (the tempo) of the beats at an even rate.

X

1 &

The verbal act of counting "one, and" over and over while clapping is a demonstration of "keeping the beat" and reciting the primary symmetrical subdivision of a beat.

Concept # 3

Now clap again, but this time alternate between saying "one" and "one, and...." The "•" mark in the notation below represents a silence, that is still felt by the musician as a pulse:

X   X

1 •   1 &

This is a demonstration of how the principle of the pulse flow underlies the beat.

Concept # 4

A beat is divisible into different densities; symmetrical subdivisions dividing the beat are typically in two, four, or eight segments.

The following notation illustrates a beat subdivided into four segments (a density of 4:1). The spoken sounds called *vocables*

"e" (ee) and "a" (ah or uh) are the standard words (like "one" and "and") used in music in the West to denote subdivision. Each word is specific to its place in the matrix.

Clap your hands as before, saying "one" and "and." Now add the "e" halfway in-between the down-beat "one" and the up-beat "and," and the "a" halfway in-between the "and," and the next "one." While you clap and recite, keep the tempo (the rate of the down-beat, the "one") even. This is a demonstration of subdividing the beat by four pulses.

$$X$$
$$1 \quad e \quad \& \quad a$$

Concept # 5

Now that you know what a beat is, and can actualize it using the basic skill of clapping and reciting subdivisions, listen to some music and clap along. Can you find the beat, clap along with it, and recite the primary subdivision ("one, and...")? Pick slower rather than faster music, as it is easier to count at slower speeds. Choose simple over complex music. Choose something you can easily clap along with at first, then progress to more difficult pieces.

Concept # 6

Rhythms (patterns of time intervals) are bound to cycles of beats, and flow along with and in relationship to the current of the beat. Feeling the beat and its density is the breath of rhythm. It is the breath of dance.

CHAPTER 7: CYCLES

With the exception of some "new music" (the term used for so-called post modern art music), most music used by belly dancers is cyclic. That is, the rhythms (*baladi, maqsum, chifte-telli*, etc.) are set in a temporal frame of a defined length—a "time cycle." A familiar example is the clock we all live our lives by (for better or worse)—it is a time cycle of twelve (twenty-four) hours in length.

In standard western musical notation, time cycles are defined by how many "beats" make up the cycle. For example, *baladi* and *maqsum* have four-beat cycles. Time cycles are indicated in music notation in various ways. In standard western notation, two numbers (one placed above the other) are used. The top number indicates how many beats are in the cycle, and the bottom number indicates the *value* (duration: an eighth-note or a quarter-note, for example) of the beat. In the notation, horizontal lines called the staves are the time line (and pitch level). Vertical lines across the staves are used to indicate measures (or bars)—a synonym for the time cycle. Given these basic notational indicators, melodies and rhythms written on the stave-lines are thus set in a context of structured time. The following example in the time cycle 4/4 shows two measures of *baladi* written in modified western notation. The dots (:) at the beginning and end are indications to repeat everything between them.

Stepping back now from the technicalities of notation, this chapter is simply about the primary concept itself: the time cycle.

Every day, we humans (and all living beings) are surrounded and physically influenced by natural circadian cycles of day/night, the phases of the moon, and the seasons. We use clocks, calendars, and other human designed cycles to organize our lives. The time cycle in music is a reflection of these experiences. The ancient classical musical scholars of Arabia, Persia, Turkey, Greece, and India used both divisive (geometry) and additive methods to design time cycles in music. Both of these methods have philosophical/metaphysical meaning, in addition to their practical application. The divisive method divides the circle as shown in #2, below. The additive method is to sequence segments of time (2s and 3s, for example), assembling them into a cycle (2 + 3 + 3 = 8).

Here is an easy way to think of a divisive time cycle in music using graphics:

1. The marks represent beats on a time line. Count as "*one, and, two, and, three, and, four, and....*" The number signifies the *down-beat*; the "and" corresponds to the halfway point between beats called the *up-beat*.

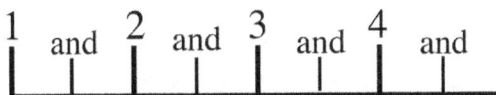

2. The line with the marks in #1 is curved around to form a circle (as in a clock).

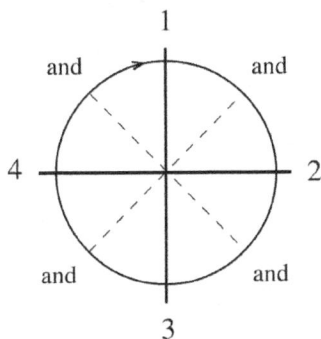

3. The following is an illustration of the basic *baladi* rhythm (<u>DT</u> •<u>T</u> D T) set around a divided circle. The dot (•) represents a "rest"—no sound.

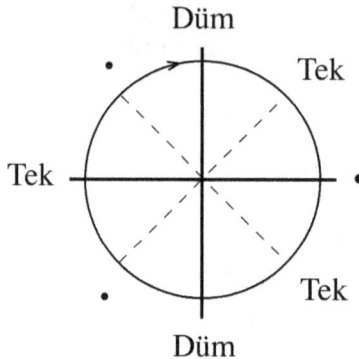

Düm

Tek

Tek

Tek

Düm

It is standard practice among musicians to use the "one"—the first beat of the cycle—as the primary reference point of the cycle. This is a learned skill, and once it is internalized, you will sense the "one."

An easy way of learning to count the beats of a cycle, and to see the form, is to use the following finger counting method adopted from Indian theory and practice. Hold your right hand palm towards your face. Use the tip of the thumb to count from the left to right on the fingertips starting with the little finger. The numbers go with the fingers; the "ands" go in-between. If you are left-handed, use the left hand but start from the index finger.

(**Hint:** If there are more than four beats in a cycle and you run out of fingers, continue from the first finger.)

Try listening to some music, preferably slow in speed, and see if you can finger-count along with the beat. Use *baladi* or *maqsum* (both common four-beat cycles). While you do this, count out loud. Watch out for shifts in the cycle between rhythms (for example between *baladi* and *chifte-telli* (*wahad e noss*) typical of Arabic cabaret orchestral music.) If you miss, get lost, whatever, back the music up and keep trying. Can you recite *baladi* or *maqsum* while finger counting? Try it!

Why learn all this? Having a fundamental understanding of musical time (the beat and cycle) will ground you in the music, allow you to hear the music on a deeper level, and will help you design your dancing. This is an enlightening experience that will really help you understand where the music is going, and its form and structure. Mastering this basic skill is also a key to learning the rhythms used in belly dance music. It will help you to dance with live musicians in the moment without having ever heard the music before because you will comprehend the beat and cycle underlying the rhythm rather than simply reacting to it.

CHAPTER 8: RHYTHM

What is rhythm? Simply put, rhythm is patterns of order and disorder using sound and silence. Rhythm has several basic attributes: It has repetition or implied repetition; it emphasizes or de-emphasizes certain sound or silences; it is fundamentally derived from speech, vocalization (e.g., the braying of donkeys), and the imitation of natural sounds (such as waves, heartbeat, and droplets) and motion (walking and running).

As civilizations grew, theory and practice regarding rhythm and musical time did too. Rhythm as devised by humans has become complex beyond its natural beginnings. Math, geometry, machines, and spiritual beliefs have all had their influence. Beat music—like that used for belly dance—is rooted in cycles of beats. In this context, rhythm is set in relationship to this formal structure. This chapter is a basic lesson in rhythm as it applies to beat music for belly dance.

As noted, repetition (or at least the human perception of it) is a fundamental aspect of rhythm. This is not to say that rhythm is endless and non-varying. Take human speech, for example. If you listen to someone speak, you will hear that while one person may have little rhythmic flow of words, another may speak in a rhythmical way. The intentional use of rhythmic speech is ancient (e.g., the Vedas). A familiar form employing specific rhythmic patterning is traditional poetry such as the limerick. The example on the next page is by Anonymous.

> "The limerick packs laughs anatomical
> In space that is quite economical,
> But the good ones I've seen
> So seldom are clean,
> And the clean ones so seldom are comical."

Other forms of poetry, while not strict with how the rhythm of the words flow, are nonetheless rhythmical and use wordplay; for example, this line from the poem "Piano" by D.H. Lawrence. Recite this and feel how the word-sounds and silences flow, and how they are accented or not.

> "Softly, in the dusk, a woman is singing to me;
> Taking me back down the vista of years, till I see
> A child sitting under the piano,
> in the boom of the tingling strings
> And pressing the small, poised feet
> of a mother who smiles as she sings."

Using basic rhythmic skill, here is a way to entrain yourself to the rhythm *maqsum* (a derivative of *baladi*) set in a cycle of four down-beats. Continue the repetition of the cycle a few times in order to get the feel of each exercise.

1. Clap a steady down-beat and recite the words. Emphasize (accent: >) the words "one" and "three." This is a simple rhythm.

>		>	
X	X	X	X
One and	Two and	Three and	Four and

2. Again, clap a steady beat and recite the next set of words, noticing that this time some are missing. Now you are reciting a more complex rhythm. Note that the spaces (silences) are as important as the sounds.

>		>	
X	X	X	X
One and	• and	Three •	Four •

3. Finally, using the same pattern as the previous example, substitute with the modern drum-tone words "dum" (the low tone) and "tek" (the high tone)—this is the *maqsum* rhythm. In this rhythmical pattern, notice there are added accents on the "and" of down-beat one, and on the down-beat "four." The emphasis of the "and" of one, and the de-emphasis of the down-beat two, creates what is called *syncopation* (the displacement of an expected beat in a series of regular beats). This is a common way to create motion in rhythm. The *tek* before the *dum* on down-beat three creates a closure of the displacement effect. Although a technical musical analysis, take a moment and think about this. This concept is at the heart of all belly dance rhythm.

> >		>	>
X	X	X	X
Dum Tek	• Tek	Dum •	Tek •

The next time you listen to some music you want to dance to, be an active listener rather than a passive or reactive one. Think about the rhythms you are hearing and how they fit with the down-beats and the time cycle. This process of listening and analysis will have a fundamental effect on your ability to dance with rhythm rather than simply to react to it. Emotion and Mind are co-aspects of consciousness, not polarities.

CHAPTER 9: A RHYTHMIC GUIDE

Underlying most pieces of music used to accompany belly dance (*danse orientale,* a.k.a. *raqs sharqi,* dance of the orient or east) is a specific rhythm. Performed by the lead percussionist (dumbek, riq, or other), each structured rhythmic pattern consists of a repeating sequence of drum-tones.

The three principle drum-tones are pitched low, medium, and high. They provide the main melodic range used by the percussionist to define a rhythm. The low and high pitches (called *dum* and *tek,* on the dumbek) are the important notes, with the mid-tones (*ta, ka*) providing color and style. Rhythmic patterns made up of specific sequences of low- and high-pitched drum-tones (re: *dum* and *tek*) are called *rhythmic modes* (*iqàat*-mode, *wazn*-measure, *dwar*-cycle, *usül*-code) in Arabic and Turkish classical theory.

The following lists of rhythms are written in simple "cipher" notation. Each pattern represents a basic form of the rhythm without ornamentation. Ornamentation and variation is what gives the basic pattern life.

To learn each rhythm, establish the time cycle first by counting and clapping over and over. For example, "one, two, three, four, one, two, three...," etc., and

Notation Key	
D = quarternotes	♩
D̲T̲ = eigthnotes	♫
D̲k̲t̲k̲ = sixteenthnotes	♬
• = rest	

then while continuing to clap the time cycle, recite the pattern. In this type of notation, underlines take the place of beams (used in standard western notation to denote density). No underline equals one quarter-note (1:1) in value. One underline = eighth-notes (2:1), and two underlines = sixteenth-notes (4:1). D = *dum,* the low tone; T = *tek,* the high tone; • = silence.

Masmudi Family

1	&	2	&	3	&	4	&	5	&	6	&	7	&	8	&
D		D		•		T		D		•		T		•	

Masmudi kabir [8-beat cycle]

1	&	2	&	3	&	4	&
D	D	•	T	D	•	T	•

Masmudi saghrir (baladi) [4-beat cycle]

1	&	2	&	3	&	4	&
D	T	•	T	D	•	T	•

Maqsum [4-beat cycle]

1	&	2	&	3	&	4	&
D	T	•	D	D	•	T	•

Sa'idi [4-beat cycle]

1	e	&	a	2	e	&	a
D	T	•	T	D	•	T	•

Fellahi [2-beat cycle]

Other fours

	1	&	2	&	3	&	4	&
Khaliji	D		.		D		.	
						T		.
Debke	D	D	T	D	D		.	
							T	.
Wahda e noss	D•TT		•DT•		D	D	T	.

Twos

	1	e	&	a	2	e	&	a
Ayyub	D	•	T	•	D		T	•
Malfuf	D	•	•	T	•	•	T	•
Karatchi	D	•	T	•	T	•	D	•

Eights

	1	&	2	&	3	&	4	&	5	&	6	&	7	&	8	&
Chiftetelli (Turkish style)	D		T	T	•		T		D		D		T		*	
Chiftetelli (Rom style)	D		•	T	•		T		D		D		T		*	
Chiftetelli (Danse Orientale style variation)	D		T	T	•	D	T		D		D		T		*	

Six

1	2	3	4	5	6
D	.	T	D	T	.

Shish Hashst (Persian six)

Seven

1	2	3	4	5	6	7
D	.	T	D	.	T	.

Kalamatiano (Greek seven)

Nine

1	2	3	4	5	6	7	8	9
D	.	T	.	D	.	T	T	T

Karshlama (Turkish, Armenian nine)

Ten

1	2	3	4	5	6	7	8	9	10
D	.	T	.	T	.	D	.	T	.

Jurjuna (Iraqi, Armenian ten)

Belly Dance Rhythm Resource

SECTION II

BASIC
RHYTHMS

North Africa, East Africa, and The Mid-East—
The Major Countries of Origin or Influence of Belly Dance Music

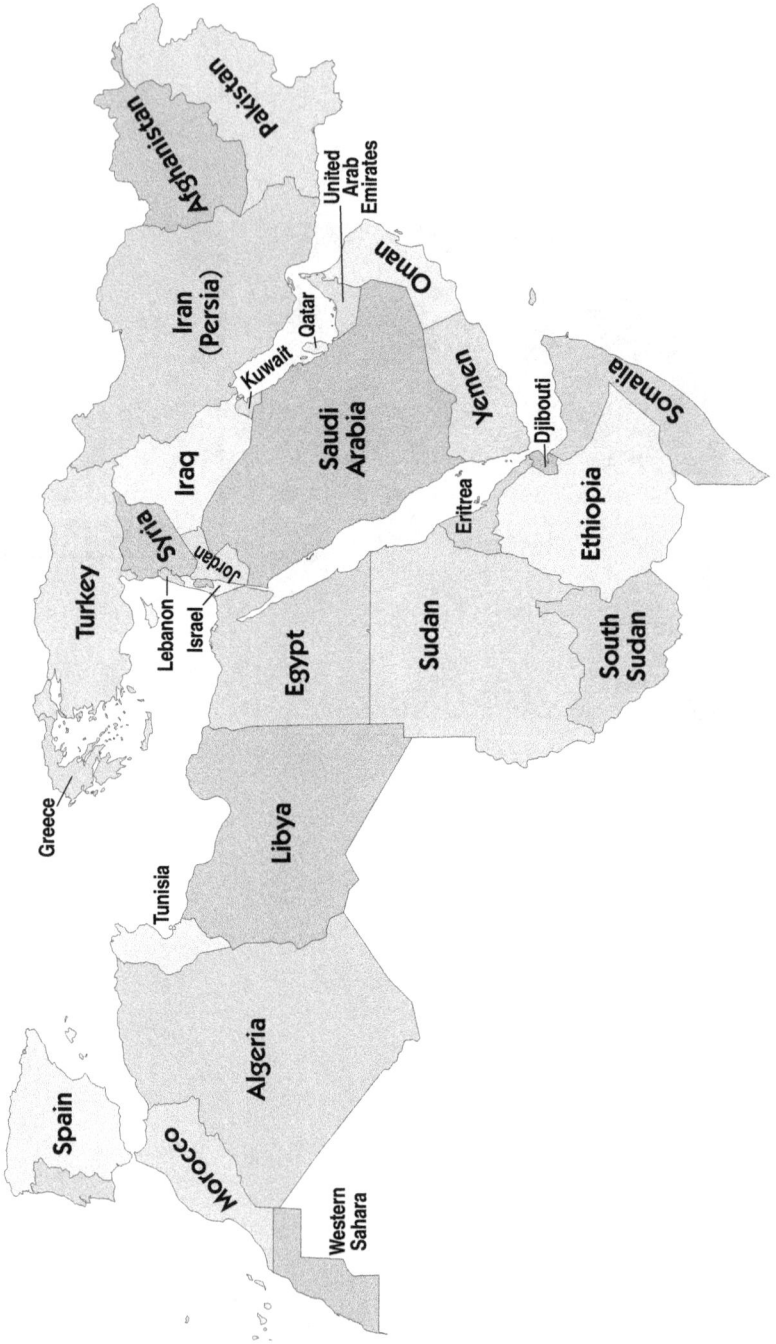

CHAPTER 10: BALADI

Baladi is, arguably, the most well-known and common of the rhythms used in Arabic popular, classical, and folk music in the present era. It is *the* basic rhythmic pattern all belly dancers should be familiar with. The Arabic word *baladi* (sometimes misspelled *beledy* or *beledi*) means "local," "rural," or "country," depending on the context of its use. The spelling *beledy* is used in the West to specifically refer to the long dress used in dance, not to the rhythm.

Baladi is a four-beat rhythm derived from an eight-beat rhythm called *masmudi kabir*—it is a half-length version. There are at least four patterns derived from *masmudi kabir* (a.k.a. *masmudi*): four-beat *masmudi saghir* (a.k.a. *baladi*), four-beat *maqsum*, two-beat *fellâhi*, and four-beat *Sa'idi*. The words *kabir* (large) and *saghir* (small) are applied as suffixes denoting the length of the time cycle (meter). The originating eight-beat rhythm is called *masmudi* since it is believed to have started among the *Masmuda*, an ancient tribal confederacy of agricultural Berbers living in northwestern Africa (the *Maghreb*). The *masmudi, maqsum, Fellâhi*, and *Sa'idi* rhythms will be discussed in other chapters of Sections II–IV.

After learning the melodo-rhythmic drum-note sequence of *baladi* as described below, can you identify it in recordings and performances? Can you say it as you dance? Remember, this drum-note sequence is the basic structure of the *baladi* pattern—drummers embellish it while keeping the structure. Another element to be aware of is that in many musical pieces, more than one rhythm is used. For example, a piece may begin in *Baladi*, shift to another rhythm, and then return. Once you

begin to recognize the basic rhythmic patterns, this will not be a confusing issue.

To learn the four-beat time-cycle foundation that *baladi* is set upon, clap (X) your hands on the *down-beat* (number) then open them on the *up-beat* (&). Say the words, "One, and, Two, and, Three, and, Four, and." Keep repeating the sequence. You are keeping time in a cycle of four beats.

X		X		X		X	
1	&	2	&	3	&	4	&

In the following notation example of *baladi*, the letters **D** = *Dum* ("doom"), the low-pitched drum-note of the dumbek; **T** = *Tek*, the high-pitched drum-note of the dumbek; and • = *silence*. On top of steady hand clapping, recite the following sequence of words and silences: *Dum Dum • Tek Dum • Tek •*. Traditional *baladi* is played at a medium pace with an emphasis on the first two *Dums* in the sequence—the second stronger than the first.

1	&	2	&	3	&	4	&
X		X		X		X	
D	D	•	T	D	•	T	•

Try saying the rhythm while listening to a piece of music with the rhythm in it. Remember, *baladi*, like many other Middle-Eastern rhythms, can be identified by its melodic low- and high-pitched drum-note sequence. Good examples to listen to are belly dance standards such as *Wahashtini, Ya Salat El Zain*, or *Zaina*.

CHAPTER 11: MAQSUM

A standard rhythm in belly dance music, *maqsum* should be familiar to the dancer. *Maqsum* (pronounced mahk-SOOM in Arabic, meaning "divided") or *düyek* in Turkish, is a common rhythm in the Middle East, like *baladi*. However, *baladi* is historically and culturally associated with Egypt and the Arabs. *maqsum*, on the other hand, has wider currency and is used in Turkish as well as Arabic music.

As noted in the previous chapter, the *baladi* pattern (D D • T D • T •) is the four-beat expression of eight-beat *masmudi kabir* (D D • T D • T •). *Masqum* is a variant of *baladi*. *Maqsum* follows almost the same sequence of drum-notes as *baladi*, with one difference: the second *Dum* in the pattern is replaced by a *Tek* (circled in the diagram below). To learn this rhythm, clap your hands on the downbeats (1, 2, 3, 4) and recite the following sequence: Dum Tek • Tek Dum • Tek •. As with *baladi*, emphasize the second drum-note—in this case, *Tek*).

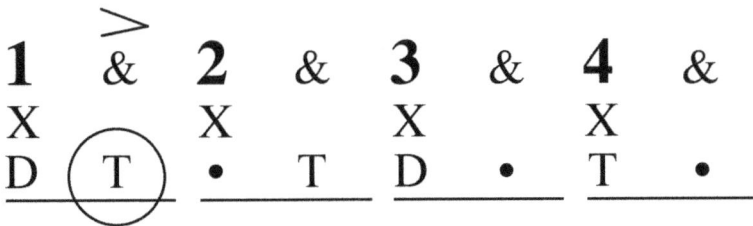

1	&	2	&	3	&	4	&
X		X		X		X	
D	T	•	T	D	•	T	•

Another important difference is that while *baladi* is traditionally played with a heavy feel and at a moderate pace, *maqsum* is played with a lighter touch and at a faster pace. Thus, in dance, movement to *baladi* tends to be earth-centered (sensual and artistic—showcase for precision technique), whereas motion to

maqsum has a less gravity-bound nature (more joyous, playful, or flirtatious—common entrance piece). These actions are interpretive and should be taken in light of the context in which the music and dance are performed (i.e., traditional, modern, or somewhere in-between).

Two examples of music with the *maqsum* rhythm are the first section of *Tamer Henna,* and the song *Shatti al-Duniya.* Keep in mind that the choice of what rhythm to play for any given realization of a piece of music is up to the musicians. Not all performers use the same rhythms. The best, and only real way to gain familiarity with any Middle-Eastern rhythm is to remember that at its core is the basic *Dum-Tek* melody. While listening to a rhythm, try to discern the *core pattern.* Clap your hands along with the beat and recite the pattern—see if it fits.

CHAPTER 12: SA'IDI

Abstracted from its roots, the *sa'idi* (pronounced, sah-EE-dee) rhythm has become favored in current Arabic pop-music. It's traditional context is ancient, and it is still practiced in modern-day Egypt. The *sa'idi* rhythm is named after the cultivated rural region of the Nile Valley between Cairo and Aswan called the Sa'id (Upper Egypt). In its original performance context, the *sa'idi* rhythm is used for the Egyptian combat dance called *tahtib*—a dance of men and horses (*kouhail*, purebred Arabian stallion). Images of this kind of activity are traceable into antiquity. The performances take place with the male dancers either standing on the ground, or on the backs of dancing horses, whirling, waving, and striking the ground with the *naboot* (a wood staff about 4 feet long). A less aggressive "stage" form of *tahtib*, called r*aks asaya* (or *assabaya*) performed by women, also employs the *sa'idi* rhythm. Most scholars concur that this version of the dance is satirical of the male *tahtib* dance. The women dancers use a small J-shaped cane called the *asaya* instead of the *naboot*. In both forms of dance, the implement (staff or cane) functions as a percussion instrument used to strike the ground or stage. The hits are timed to either coincide with or against the rhythm's accents.

The *sa'idi* rhythm is traditionally played outdoors on loud instruments. The *narahsan*, a big two-sided bass-drum (a.k.a. *tabl al baladi*), is held on a strap around the neck and played with sticks—the right hand striking bass tones with a rounded beater, and the left hand tapping out complex overtone-saturated treble drum-notes with a long, thin, dowel. The melody is played on double-reed oboes called the *mizmar sa'idi*. In a typical *mizmar* group there is a lead player with a second player mimicking

the first's melody (heterophony), and at least one or two drone players. The dumbek and a large tambourine called the *mazhar* are sometimes used as auxiliary percussion along with the *narahsan*.

The diagram below compares *baladi*, *maqsum* and *sa'idi*. *Sa'idi* is characterized by the two sequential *Dums* (circled in the illustration) in the middle of the cycle, not at the beginning like *baladi*.

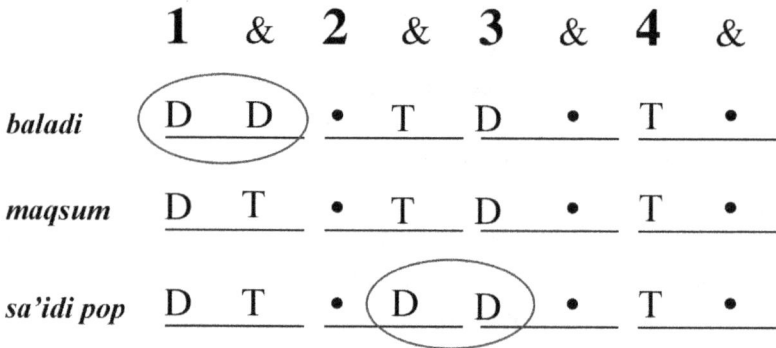

	1	**&**	**2**	**&**	**3**	**&**	**4**	**&**
baladi	D	D	•	T	D	•	T	•
maqsum	D	T	•	T	D	•	T	•
sa'idi pop	D	T	•	D	D	•	T	•

There are variations of *sa'idi*. In example one, the initial (and expected) two drum-tone sequence of *Dum Tek* is inverted to be *Tek Dum*. It is typical of the traditional style played on the *narahsan*.

sa'idi trad.	T	D	•	D	D	•	T	•

In example two, an extra *Dum* is added on the "and" of beat one. It is a typical of a pop music variation.

sa'idi var.	D	D	•	D	D	•	T	•

The illustration below shows the *sa'idi* group in Time Unit Box (TUBs)-style notation.

Sa'idi (4)

Sa'idi traditional

Sa'idi variation 1

The *sa'idi* rhythm is very much like one of the standard dance rhythms found in western rock 'n roll. See the drumset notation illustration below. Translated to the dumbek, it is D • T D D • T •. (Read *Dum* as a bass drum and *Tek* as a snare drum in this example.) The difference is that in the rock pattern (example one), the first *Tek* is set on beat number two instead of the "and" of beat one as it is in *sa'idi* (example two).

Dancers often confuse *sa'idi* with *baladi* since they are very similar, having two *Dums* together. As a consequence, the zill pattern accents played by the dancer are for *baladi* rather than *sa'idi*. Although counterpoint is a relevant strategy for a zillist (and should be a part of their musical vocabulary), making the accents flow with the structure of the rhythmic mode creates a strong form. Knowledgeable musical interaction by a zillist with a *dumbek/darabukka/tabla* player makes for a far more interesting and varied performance than galloping zills for every song the same way each time. For extensive information and sound examples of zill patterns see: HTTP://WWW.CYBERLEPSY. COM/ZILLS.HTML. By knowing where the "One" is in the time cycle, and where the two *Dums* go, the differences between the two rhythms are clear (iterated above).

To familiarize yourself with the differences between *baladi* and *sai'di,* try listening to some Arabic music. Can you identify *sa'idi* from the other rhythms? Although *sa'idi* is the traditional rhythm played for *tahtib* and *raks asaya*, other rhythms including *baladi* and *maqsum* are also used. Keep the structure of the drum-tone sequence (see example above) in mind while listening to the music. Can you hear the pattern? Find the "One" in the time cycle and recite the *sa'idi* drum-tone sequence. Even though a CD label says it's a Sa'idi album, the rhythm may not be *sa'idi*. Listen carefully. The following examples of *sa'idi* should be helpful in identifying *sa'idi*. An excellent example of traditional *sai'di* is Hossam Ramzy's *Kouhail* CD. As for modern *sa'idi* applications, listen to Arabic popular music, it's everywhere. However, some good examples may be heard in the popular singer Amir Diab's recordings of "Hikayatey," "Bahibak Aktar," and "Betuhashney" on his *Amarain* CD. "Ala Nar" by the Sami Nossair Orchestra is a good example of orchestral *sa'idi* pop. Clips of these songs are available, free to listen, online at various music websites.

CHAPTER 13: AYYUB

The *ayyub* (eye-YOUB) rhythm, also spelled *ayoub*, and *eyyub* (a Turkish *arabesk üsul*), is widespread throughout the Middle East, and is applied in a variety of settings such as *debke* (a line-dance) and *zar* (a healing ritual)—both these forms of rhythm and dance will be discussed in later articles in this series. Although there are folk and urban variants of *ayyub*, the urban form, usually felt and notated as a two-beat pattern, is the most familiar to belly dancers. It is interesting to note that the proper name *Ayyub,* refers to a descendant of the Prophet Ibrahim (equated with the biblical *Job*)—linked with the virtue of patience. Whether or not the name is associated with the rhythm is unknown to the author—it provides a potential research topic.

The following example shows the standard two-beat short-form used in the *danse orientale* community. It is used in dance suites in fast sections, as a transitional pattern, and sometimes in alternation or combination with *fellâhi* (covered in "Chapter 25: Fellâhi" of Section IV). Ayyub is very similar to *fellâhi*, differing by only one drum-note: the *Tek* on the "e" of beat one. Ayyub is often subjectively referred to as a strident and catchy rhythm inspiring strong and vigorous movement. There is an emphasis on the "a" of beat one and the "and" of beat two (the same as *fellâhi*).

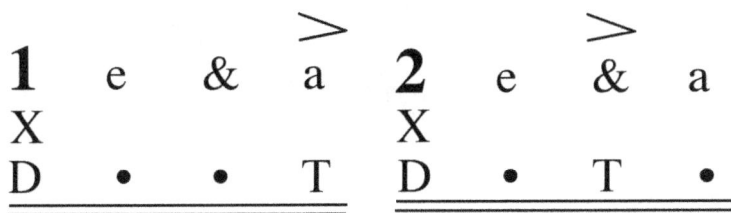

			>				>	
1	e	&	a	**2**	e	&	a
X				X			
D	•	•	T	D	•	T	•

A useful example of the rhythm alone can be found on Issam Houshan's *The Dancing Drum* CD. The rhythm in performance context can be heard in the opening section of *Tabeli Ya Susu* on Susu Pampanin's *Dancing Drums* CD, and throughout *Gahwa Dance Time* on Cairo Caravan's *Belly Dance with Dina* CD. Remember, core patterns are often ornamented—*ayyub* is not an exception. Clap your hands to the downbeats, listen carefully, and you will hear it.

CHAPTER 14: MALFUF

The rhythm *malfuf* (pronounced mal-FOOF) is common to folk and popular Arabic music. It is also found in Greek and Turkish music. The core rhythm 3 3 2, is also found in the Saudi *khalīji* rhythm, although with different drum-tones. The pattern 3 3 2 is also a primary rhythmic characteristic of the music of the Hispanic west and the African-Arabic-Spanish hybrid called *Andalusian*. The name *malfuf* is translated from Arabic as "wrapped" or "spun around" in reference to stuffed, rolled cabbage leaves found in the Mediterranean region. Why would a rhythm be named after a stuffed cabbage roll? Other than the fanciful reference to the "rolling" quality of the rhythm, it is unknown why.

Used for belly dance, *malfuf* functions both as a rhythmic device for entrances and exits, and as a principle rhythm. *Malfuf* is set in a cycle of two quarter-notes, each subdivided into four sixteenth-notes at 1:4, making a total of eight pulses. *Malfuf*, like most of the other rhythms of the Middle East used for belly dance, can be identified by its "melody."

Malfuf's drum-tone melody is D • • T • • T •.

cycle downbeats:	1				2			
clap:	X				X			
sixteenthnotes:	1	2	3	4	5	6	7	8
accents:	>			>			>	
count:	1	e	&	a	2	e	&	a
drumtone pattern:	D	•	•	T	•	•	T	•

The asymmetrical additive structure of *malfuf* is defined by its segments: 3 + 3 + 2. In the example below, notice that the prime accent of the first segment lines up with the main down-beat of the cycle, but the other two do not. This rhythmic tension is called *syncopation* or *cross-rhythm*, in which an expected beat is played in an unexpected place. For example, instead of on the down-beat, the note is played offset to the up-beat (the "and" instead of the "one"). This phenomenon is a principle engine of rhythmic motion in music and dance. Human bodies are symmetrical forms, our physical motions are predominated by movements up and down, side to side, back and forth, and so on. *Malfuf*, as a syncopated rhythm, causes the body to "lose balance" and thus induces motion. Taken as a set of eight, the eight pulses are grouped into three segments of three (3) + three (3) + two (2).

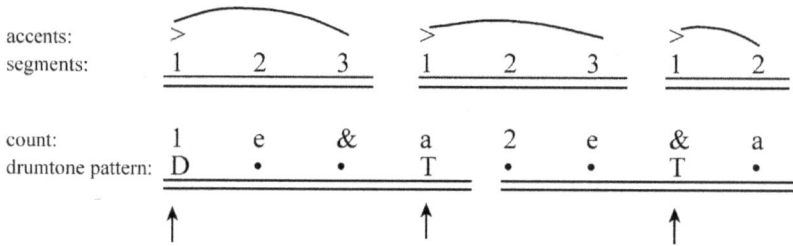

accents:	>			>			>	
segments:	1	2	3	1	2	3	1	2
count:	1	e	&	a	2	e	&	a
drumtone pattern:	D	•	•	T	•	•	T	•

Noted above, the 3 3 2 pattern as a rhythmic core is found throughout western Hispanic music as well as Spanish and Andalusian music. In Mexican music, for example, it can be heard as a guitar chord rhythm in popular songs such as "Guantanamara." The same rhythm appears in Spanish *flamènco*. In Cuban and Salsa music, the *clavé* pattern (the rhythmic foundation) is based upon a rhythm called the *tresillo*; the first half of which has the same pattern found in *malfuf*.

Rhythmic core pattern (tresillo)

3-2 son clavé (cinquillo)

A variant of *tresillo* called *cinquillo* (with five accents counted: 1 • 3, 1 • 3, 1 •) is inherent in North American *boogie woogie*. Both the three and five variant are found in *rock 'a billy* and other early *rock 'n roll* forms. A great example is the bass-line in Elvis' song "Hound Dog." The 3 3 2 pattern is also found in some Asian music. It is interesting to note that 3 3 2 is also the Euclidean rhythm E(3, 8).[1] The form 3 3 2 seems to be one of the most widespread rhythmic patterns among humans on Earth.

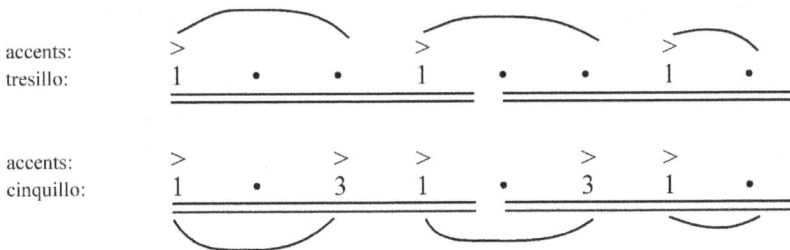

Tresillo and Cinquillo written in cipher notation

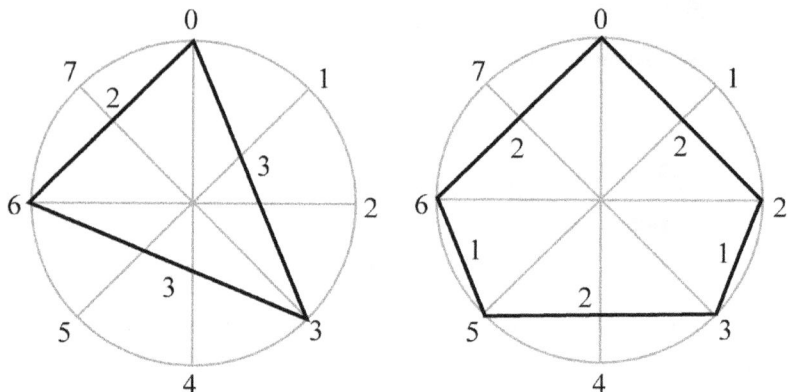

Euclidean diagrams for tresillo E 3,8) and cinquillo E (5,8)[1]

Some recorded examples of *malfuf* can be heard on Hossam Ramzy's *Baladi Plus (Egyptian Dance Music)* CD, #7 "Malfuf Ala Westi"; Nourhan Sharif's *Arabic Rhythms* CD, vol. 1, #1 "Malfouf"; and Issam Houshan's *The Dancing Drum* CD, #7 "Malfoof."

Clap your hands to the down-beats and feel the cross-rhythm (explained in "Chapter 36: Cross-Rhythm" in Section V). Better yet, understand the rhythm and *dance* to it!

---

[1] Euclidean diagram adapted from: Toussaint, Godfried "The *Euclidean* Algorithm Generates Traditional Musical Rhythms," in the *Proceedings of BRIDGES: Mathematical Connections in Art, Music and Science*, Banff, Alberta, Canada, July 31–August 3, 2005, pp. 47–56.

CHAPTER 15: MASMUDI—THE "MOTHER RHYTHM"

The eight-beat cycle pattern called *masmudi kabir* (large) is believed to have derived from a rhythm among the *Masmuda*, an ancient tribal confederacy of agricultural Berbers living in the western part of north Africa. Western Arab court musicians in 13TH century Morocco and Tunisia first adapted the rhythm to the Classical vocal suite called the *muwashahat* (Arabic for "girdled"). An alternate name for the rhythm is *masmudi taweel*, referring to the three *Dums* in its sequence (see diagram on the next page). *Masmudi* (common name, pronounced mas-MOODY) is identical to the *baladi* rhythm, a.k.a. *masmudi saghir* (small), but is spread over a cycle of eight beats instead of four beats (two measures or bars). *Baladi*, and *masmudi kabir's* other derivative rhythms, *maqsum*, and *sa'idi*, have been discussed in previous chapters. Another derivative *masmudi* rhythm, *Fellâhi*, will be covered in a Chapter 25 of Section IV.

In modern music suites played by Arabic light-classical orchestras that accompany popular singers such as Fairuz and Um Kalthum, *masmudi* functions as a contrasting time-cycle alternate during slow movements. For example, it is placed between segments of the four-beat cycle of *maqsum* or *baladi*, creating a kind of time-stretch effect. In modern music for *danse orientale*, *masmudi* is used as one of several expressive, slow to medium tempi, dance rhythms such as *chiftetelli* or *Arabic boléro* for veil and floor-work. It is also used in this context as a time-stretch effect, as described above, as well. The tempo at which *masmudi* is played ranges from 80 bpm (typical) to 120 bpm (less common), depending upon the situation.

The following example illustrates the core *masmudi* rhythm. Sometimes the second *Dum* (beat 2) is left out as a variation.

1	2	3	4	5	6	7	8
D	D	•	T	D	•	T	•

The next example shows one way of decorating the principle drum-tones (marked by accents) of *masmudi*.

>	>		>	>		>	
1	2	3	4	5	6	7	8
D	D	tktk	T	Dtk	tkt	Tktk	t

An example (towards the middle of the piece) of the classical use of *masmudi* is found in "Khatwet Habiby" (Footsteps of My Love) by Muhammad Abd al-Wahhab in *EGYPT: The Music of Islam, Vol. 1: Al-Qahirah—Classical Music*. An example of a more modern way it is used for belly dance may be heard in "Escape From Cairo" (about a third into the piece) by Mohammad Al Hasan Abo Abid on *Master of Egyptian Bellydance*. A song made famous by Um Kalthoum called "Hadiyi Laylati" (Gift of the Night) is another example of the use of *masmudi*. It has been recorded by many artists, including the unique Arabic electric guitarist Omar Khorshid. Western interpretive ensembles tend to use *masmudi* for longer segments, if not throughout the entire piece. Recordings of drum patterns (including *masmudi* and many others) are available for dancers in which the rhythm is repeated, allowing the dancer to learn rhythms abstracted without the melody parts. There are many such rhythm practice recordings available. It is recommended that dancers use these, reciting the pattern while they practice in order to fix it in their memories.

CHAPTER 16: MASMUDI'S INFLUENCE

Rhythmic modes in belly dance music are the core structures used to generate patterns. These patterns provide a basis over which the musician creates rhythmic variation. The rhythmic mode called *masmudi* (a.k.a *wazn masmudi kabir*) is used herein to demonstrate how one pattern can be used to generate several distinct rhythmic melodies. Although *masmudi* has been discussed and compared in other chapters in this collection, here the rhythm is shown with a visual notation method that is useful to see both the pitch orientation (that defines a particular variation), and its relationship to the cycle.

To begin, here is a brief review of the fundamentals of musical time. Rhythm, a pattern of accented and unaccented sounds and spaces of various durations, is not bound by measured time in its natural state. In a musical application, however, it is. The standard method is to bind the rhythm to a repeating cycle of equal beats or pulses. These terms are interchangeable, but the term "beat" implies a hierarchical level of importance over "pulse" (the fundamental unit of time in music).

In the following illustration, a line of eight equal pulses represented by dots has been isolated.

The line of pulses is bent around upon itself to form a circle representing a cycle of eight.

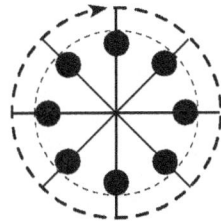

By using *accents* (a stress on a sound, making it louder than the others) the eight-pulse cycle is defined herein into two possible cycles: 8 and 4. In each diagram, the lines denoting the divisions are darkened to imply that they are accented. The pulses in-between the accented beats of the cycle of four are felt as subdivisions. Count out the numbers, clapping on the beat (indicated by numbers) for these two cycles. These two cycles provide an underlying time form for the analysis of the generative rhythmic mode *masmudi*.

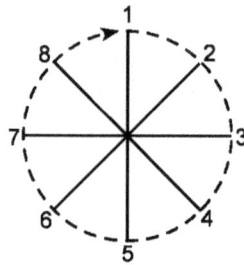

An eight-beat cycle counted ONE, TWO, THREE, FOUR, FIVE, SIX, SEVEN, EIGHT.

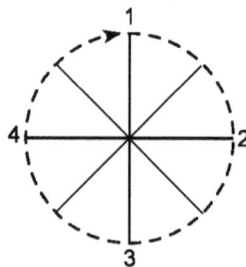

A four-beat cycle counted ONE, and, TWO, and, THREE, and, FOUR, and ("and" is the subdivision).

The simple notation method known as TUBs (time-unit boxes) is an easy way for non-musicians to see cycle and rhythm. In this method, each box represents an equal unit of duration. The following example shows eight time-units.

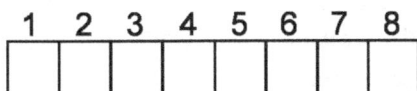

1	2	3	4	5	6	7	8

The primary generative rhythmic mode for *masmudi* abstracted from pitch is shown below, set in a cycle of eight beats. In the notation, a dot (•) is used to mark a sound. A box without a dot is a silent space. In performance practice, the spaces between the primary rhythm are decorated with various ornamentations according to tradition. When hearing *masmudi* performed, listen for the primary rhythm.

•	•		•	•		•	

Masmudi kabir
primary rhythmic mode pattern

As suggested above, in performance practice (relative to music theory), a simple melody using a low tone (*Dum*) and a high tone (*Tek*) is used to characterize individual patterns. Both *masmudi* and *baladi* (the first variant) have the same melody. However, *masmudi* is played to a count of an eight-beat cycle, whereas *baladi* (the same rhythmic melody) is played to the count of a four-beat cycle.

1	2	3	4	5	6	7	8
D	D	•	T	D	•	T	•

Masmudi

1	&	2	&	3	&	4	&
D	D	•	T	D	•	T	•

Baladi

Tek			●		●		
Dum	●	●		●			

Masmudi kabir/saghir
Baladi

Using the same core *masmudi* rhythm, three more identifiable rhythmic-melodies can be generated (in addition to *baladi*) by changing the pitches: *maqsum*, and two versions of *sa'idi*. These three variants are set in a cycle of four (see previous page for explanation).

Tek		●		●		●	
Dum	●				●		

Maqsum

Tek		●				●	
Dum	●			●	●		

Sa'idi

Tek	●			●		●	
Dum		●			●		

Sa'idi variation

As can be seen, *masmudi* is the source pattern (mode) from which, by varying the length of the cycle and changing the pitch but not rhythm, other distinct melodic patterns can be made. These same processes are applicable to any core rhythmic mode and cycle that is used in belly dance. As an exercise to improve your ability to perceive and feel the rhythms you dance to, clap your hands and find the basic beat of the cycle. Once you establish it, listen for the core rhythm—it will be repeated by the musicians (most importantly, the drummer).

CHAPTER 17: CHIFTETELLI

The *chiftetelli* (shifteh-TELL-ee) rhythm, set in an eight-beat cycle, is well known in the belly dance community. Dancers use *chiftetelli* to express sensuous motion, and to display their skill with swords, veils, or floor-work. However, there is more than one way to play it (slow or fast) or dance it (solo or pairs), and the name is not always equated with the rhythm.

Even though most rhythms played on the dumbek are repetitive rhythmic melodies made of the low-pitched drum-tone *Dum* and the high-pitched drum-tone *Tek*, the *chiftetelli* rhythmic "melody" (Dum TekTek • Tek Tek Dum Dum Tek •), as played on the dumbek to accompany belly dance, is distinctive. Many western dumbek drummers tend to play *chiftetelli* with less variation than for other rhythms. It is also typical, for example, for the bass player in a nightclub ensemble to realize the pattern as a static melody without variation. This is different than the method used for other rhythms (e.g. *maqsum*) where the bassist or drummer moves the melody notes around while still keeping the rhythm "relatively" intact. Another noticeable characteristic of the *chiftetelli* rhythm is its tempo—ranging from quite slow to fast.

The *chiftetelli* rhythm is accepted by most scholars as being an imitation of the style of playing used on certain stringed and woodwind instruments—which instrument, is debatable. A compound word, *chiftetelli* is made of two components: chifte and telli. *Chifte* (çifte) is a Turkish word meaning "double," "couple," "pair," "duet," and so on, and *telli* (also Turkish) means "wire," "string," "fiber," "chord," "thread," and so on. A literal translation of *chiftetelli* is "double string."

One of the most common opinions is that the rhythm is an emulation of the traditional playing style used on the seven-stringed (sets of two + two + three) plucked (by finger picking or plectrum) long-necked lute Turkish instrument called *baglama saz*. Melodies are played on the two double-string sets, alternating with a rhythmic drone played on the triple set of strings. Variants of this instrument under different names are in use in Persian, Kurdish, Armenian, Syrian, Iraqi, and Balkan music. The *baglama saz* was a premier instrument of the Turkish Ottomans.

Another stringed instrument, the small three-stringed, pear-shaped bowed fiddle of Cretan Greece (and found in the Dodecanese islands and the Aegean Archipelago), called the *lyra* (LEE-rah), is also thought to have had originating influence upon the *chiftetelli* rhythm. The *lyra* is an ancestor of the medieval Byzantine instrument of the same name, and is the probable ancestor of some European bowed instruments. The traditional style of bowing the *lyra* uses one string for the melody, and the two other strings (one higher, the other lower in pitch) as rhythmic unstopped drones.

Although *chiftetelli* suggests a string instrument, various other theories have been put forth. The name *chifte* also may refer to paired wind instruments played with similar melodo-rhythmic patterning (melody + drone). One instrument used in this way is the *kaval (caval)* or *dzamara* (Arabic zamara, meaning "to blow" or "play"), an end-blown flute played in Azerbaijan, Turkey, Bulgaria, Macedonia, Kosovo, southern Serbia, northern Greece, southern Romania, and Armenia. Associated with mountain shepherds (predating and outside of any specific nationality), the *kaval*, like many others (including the *lyra*), migrated into the instrumentarium of urban musicians. Paired *kaval* are played

with one musician performing the lead melody, while the other musician executes the rhythmic alternating drone (with two-note drones similar to those played on the *baglama saz* and *lyra*). The pair can also be played by one person. A version of the instrument called the *chifte kaval* is an example of two bound together, as one compound instrument, with string, sticks, or a carved block of wood.

The word *chifte* sometimes erroneously refers to paired end-blown reed instruments, but such instruments are not common in the areas where the *kaval* is found. Two reed instruments with similar alternating melody/drone playing styles are the *arghul* (ar-GHOOL), a compound double-pipe Arabic single-reed clarinet), and the *mizmar* (a double-reed oboe-like woodwind with connections to the Turkish *zurna*, a type of shawm with Chinese connections) played in pairs or groups by several musicians. Their relationship to the *chiftetelli* is dubious.

The general theory among ethnomusicologists, supporting the hybridization of the word and rhythm, is that the *chiftetelli* was brought by people living in the Anatolian region into mainland Greece through Smyrna, an important trade center and migration route between the Aegean and Anatolia, now called Izmir. Smyrna is at the end of a deep inlet of the Aegean Sea at the mouth of the river Hernus on the west coast of Anatolia (now Turkey). Greeks, Roma, Turks, and Armenians, among others, all claim some connection to the rhythm, making any clear foundation of *chiftetelli*'s origin—by instrument or though culture—obscure.

The *chiftetelli* rhythm in Turkey is used for social dances for couples at weddings and other similar gatherings. In the late 1800s and early 1900s, it was adapted by urban and Roma musicians into the repertoire of rhythms for *danse orientale*.

Note that the Greeks use the term *tsifteteli* (one "l") as a synonym for solo belly dancing (Arabic *raks sharqi* or *danse orientale*). This can be confusing, since traditional *tsifteteli* is a social dance mutually improvised by a man and woman, rather than a staged solo dance. Greek *tsifteteli* rhythms include the full range of patterns available, not just the *chiftetelli* pattern.

As a result of its mixed heritage, there is a gamut of *chiftetelli* variants from folk to urban, based upon geographical-cultural region:

1. The northern-style, inclusive of Turkish, Greek, and Armenian music, is set in a cycle of eight.

Northern
(Greek, Turkish, Rom, Armenian)

1	2	3	4	5	6	7	8
D	T T	• T T	D	D	T	•	
D	• T	• T	D	D	T	•	

2. The southern (Arabic) style is set in a cycle of four. The Arabic *wahda e nous* (one and a half) or *dar e nous* (hit and a half) compresses the rhythm into four instead of eight beats.

Southern
(Arabic: *wahda e nous*, "one & a half" or *dar e nous*, "hit & a half"

1	2	3	4
D T T	• D T	D D	T •

The international *danse orientale* style of Europe and the U.S.A. is set in a cycle of eight. The westernized *danse orientale* version is a hybrid of all of the above, illustrated on the following page.

Western *Danse Orientale variants*

1	2	3	4	5	6	7	8
D	T T	• T	T	D	D	T	•
D	D T	• D	T	D	D	T	•
D	D T	• D	T	D	T	T	•
D	T T	• D	T	D	T	T	•

Tempo and Cycle

The rate of the downbeats—the tempo—affects the way *chiftetelli* is counted, and the way it is notated. *Chiftetelli* can be played slowly (100± bpm; western fusion *danse orientale*) to medium quick (130± bpm; Arabic) to fast (138± bpm; typical in Roma music). Slow *chiftetelli* is written in an eight-beat cycle; medium and fast *chiftetelli* is written in a four-beat cycle.

The tempo at which the rhythm is played also effects its realization by the percussionist. At slow speeds, dense ornamentation is easier, and therefore is favored by *danse orientale* drummers. As the tempo gets faster, the so-called *salient* beats (the pulse felt as the down-beat) counted as eight down-beats to a cycle dissolve into four down-beats to a cycle. By raising or lowering the tempo, one can shift back and forth between the long or short count, and the density of ornamentation. Tempo is equated with emotion by dancers. Fast tempi inspire fast moves and "joyfulness," and slow tempi inspire a focused intensity of expression often enhanced by the dancer with devices such as the veil or sword. The slow tempo, "sinuous" expression of *chiftetelli* is the most well known to Western dancers.

Melodo-Rhythmic Variation

Chiftetelli, like many Middle-Eastern dance rhythms, is inherently static (a reiterated pattern). In traditional folk and classical performance, there is often little to no variation to the pattern. Without any ornamentation, however, *chiftetelli* can become tedious and stagnant. The modern *danse orientale* style uses variation more than any other type of *chiftetelli.*

Northern (Greek, Turkish, Armenian, Roma)
Classic

	1	2	3	4	5	6	7	8
$\frac{8}{?}$ ‖ D		T T	•	T T	D	D	T	• ‖

The Northern classic chiftetelli is the standard melodo-rhythmic model.

The rhythmic grouping in the Northern Roma style of *chiftetelli,* emphasizes a distinct 3 + 3 + 2 shape to the first half (first four beats) of the rhythm. Tempi range upwards of 135±—a fast and lively dance for weddings. Although the rhythm is traditionally played as a static iteration, the 3 + 3 + 2 aspect creates an interesting cross-rhythmic feel, which is improvised against by the melody players. In the illustration below, the pattern is written in a cycle of eight, but should be played as if it were in a cycle of four. In other words, at a fast tempo, the salient beats are felt as a cycle of four.

Roma

		1	2	3	4	5	6	7	8
		a				b			
written:	$\frac{8}{?}$ ‖	D •	• T	• •	T •	D •	D •	T •	• • ‖
		3		3		2			
played as:	$\frac{4}{?}$	1		2		3		4	

The Southern (Arabic) style, *wahda e nous,* is almost always played fast, hence is always notated in a cycle of four beats. It is similar to the Roma *chiftetelli* in this regard, but does not have the emphasis on the 3 + 3 + 2 shape in the first half of the rhythm. A *Dum* (circled in the notation) is sometimes substituted for the *tek* on the "and" of down-beat three. The rhythm is traditionally played as a static iteration with little ornamentation.

Southern (Arabic: *wahda e nous,* or *dar e nous*)

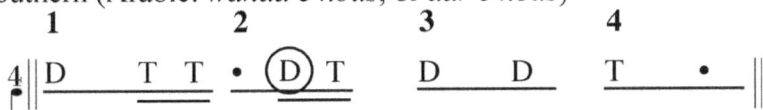

	1				2			3			4	
$\frac{4}{4}\|$	D		T	T	•	(D)	T	D		D	T	• $\|$

As already noted, the classic Northern pattern is followed as the principle model in *danse orientale.* In the following examples, typical *danse orientale* variations on the core melodo-rhythmic pattern are illustrated. This type of variation is standard in *danse orientale* performance. For comparison, example **a)** is the classic *chiftetelli* pattern. In example **b)**, a *Dum* is substituted on the "and" of beat three (like in the Arabic style), and a *Tek* is substituted for the standard *Dum* on beat six. In examples **c)** and **d)**, *Dum* replaces *Tek*.

Western *Danse Orientale variants*

		1	2	3	4	5	6	7	8
a.	D	T	T	•	T	T	D	D	T	•
b.	D	T	T	•	(D)	T	D	(T)	T	•
c.	D	(D)	T	•	(D)	T	D	(T)	T	•
d.	D	(D)	T	•	(D)	T	(D)	D	T	•

Alternation and the "Empty Beat"

The alternation of cycles of slow tempo *chiftetelli* is used as a way of enhancing the dramatic arc of the slow-tempo dance suite segment—in which dancers employ their sword(s) or veil(s). The following is a typical example showing the classic form alternated with a *danse orientale* variation.

‖: D   T T • T T   D   D   T   • |

D   T T • (D) T   D   (T)   T   • :‖

A special feature of slow realizations of *chiftetelli*, is the "empty beat," which occurs on the eighth beat of the time cycle. It is an interval of no sound—a "rest" in the rhythm. The standard alternation method in *danse orientale* style is to play one iteration of the rhythm without ornamentation on the "empty beat," and then in the second iteration add a riff on the eighth beat.

1	2	3	4	5	6	7	8
D	T T	• T	T	D	D	T	•

The following two examples show typical "riffs" that can be placed in the "empty beat" space:

a triplet: $\overset{3}{t\,t\,t}$

a roll: t t t t t t t t   or   t t t t t t t t

As the dance-suite segment progresses, the drummer increases the density and complexity of the embellishment of the rhythm, reaching a peak, and then dramatically reduces back to the simple form without, or with little, embellishment at all.

Conclusions

The *chiftetelli* rhythm is a mimic of the two-pitched rhythmic drones used in traditional string and wind instrumental performance. Its name—"paired" or "double" "strings"—reinforces the characteristic. The three general styles of *chiftetelli* are based upon regional commonality. The Northern (Turkey, Greece, Armenia, Roma) form is considered to be the classic melodo-rhythmic model for all other versions. The Northern style is the most varied in tempi and structure. The Southern (Arabic) form is similar to the quick Northern Roma style, but is played at a moderate tempo. In the slow modern *danse orientale* style, percussionists tend to combine traditions. The tempo effects the way the dancer emotes to the rhythm—fast tends towards a joyful expression, slower tends towards a focused, intense, and sensuous expression. Variation drumming techniques used to enhance the dramatic arc of the section of the dance suite in which it is used, include drum-note substitution and rhythmic fills on the eighth "empty" beat.

Recorded Examples:

1. Turkish examples can be heard on *Tzigane: The Gypsy Music of Turkey*, Erköse Ensemble, CD 3010, CMP Records, "Bahriye Ciftellisi"; on *Art of Zakari Khan*, Anatolian Ensemble, CD HMC1180, Hollywood Music Center, 2002, "Mevlana Dance"; and on *Masters of Turkish Music*, CD 1051, Rounder Records, "Chiftetelli."

2. Recordings of Greek *chiftetelli* are difficult to find. An old LP example is on *Belly Dance!* by Chris Kalogerson & His Ensemble Sharqi, 1979, "Tsifteteli El Greco."

3. An Armenian *chiftetelli* can be heard on *A Thousand And One Nights,* John Bilezikjian, CD 91001, Dantz Records, Hollywood Music Center, 2002, "Chifte Telli."

4. A demonstration of Arabic *wahad e noss* is found on *Arabic Rhythms vol. 1*, Nourhan Sharif, CD, Egyptian Academy of Dance, "Chiftetelli."

5. Examples of western-style *danse orientale chiftetelli* with ornamentation are found on recordings by ensembles such as *Solace, Light Rain, Desert Wind,* and *Brothers of the Baladi.*

Belly Dance Rhythm Resource

SECTION III

COMPLEX
RHYTHMS

Greece, The Balkans, Asia-Minor, Iraq, and Iran—
Origins and Influences of Complex Rhythms

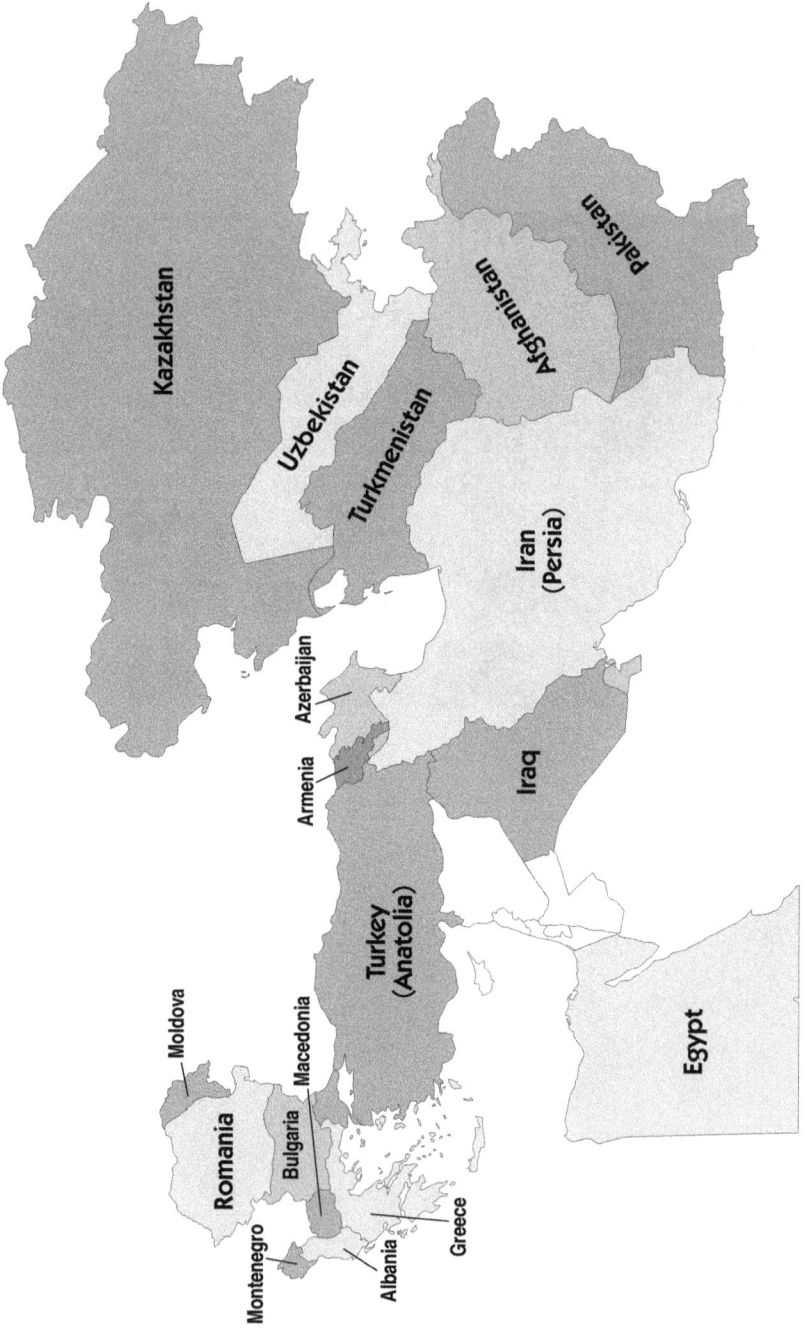

CHAPTER 18: KARSHLAMÁ (9/8 RHYTHM)

Karshlamá (karsh-lah-MAH—Turkish-Armenian, *karsh*, "face to face") or *karsilamas* (kar-see-LAH-mas—Greek, *antikry*, "facing")—which is it? The name of the rhythm and/or dance is based upon the region it comes from. Thus, for Turkish region versions, *karshlamá*; and for Greek region versions, *karsilamas* (or *antikrystos)*. They are both nine-beat-cycle rhythms (see below), and they are both socializing dances in which couples face each other as they move. Variations of the dance (in both cultures) include male- or female-only versions. The traditional setting is a wedding party, a birthday, or a general gathering. The embellishment of the basic drum-tones of the rhythm by the dancer(s) may include handkerchief flourishes, spinning, jumping, kneeling, and synchronized punctuations with the hands slapping on the ground or body. These moves are a playful interaction and competition in the social setting. Abstracted from the original, the cabaret-style *karshlamá* (*karsilamas*) 9/8 rhythm is danced as a solo.

The exact origin of the nine-beat *karshlamá* or *karsilamas* rhythm is hazy. One possible source is believed to be the *zeibékiko*, a slow and heavy (strong) feeling nine-beat-cycle rhythm and dance of the *Zeibek* people on the western coast of Turkey (Anatolia). A fast version of rhythm known as *karshlamá* is associated with Turkish Gypsy Rom wedding party musicians. Armenians use their version of *karshlamá* as one of their principle traditional rhythms in music. The Greek *karsilamas* variant is believed to come from the western region of Kutahya in Thrace, and Macedonia (north of Greece), and an association is held with the Mytilene Port on the Isle of Lesbos. The *danse orientale* version of *karshlamá/karsilamas* is sometimes referred to as "9/8," and is the most common type used by belly dancers.

When notating rhythms, the beat-value chosen for the time-cycle is set relative to the tempo at which it is typically performed. Fast-tempo rhythms can be set in a sixteenth-note beat value, whereas medium tempo rhythms can be set at an eighth- or quarter-note level. Slow rhythms are usually set in quarter-note or half-note value levels. *Karshlamá/karsilamas* notated in a nine-beat cycle at the sixteenth-note level = 9/16; eighth-notes = 9/8; or quarter-note beats = 9/4. The western *dance orientale* version is translated to fit into a nine-beat cycle using a beat-value level of eighth-notes—hence the demarcation of the meter "9/8."

On a structural level, the *karshlamá/karsilamas* rhythm is an accented sequence of even- and odd-numbered cells of beats. This structure is referred to in Turkish music as being an *aksak* or "limping" type of rhythm. There are many examples of *aksak* rhythms throughout the Turkish, Greek, and Balkan regions. It is unknown whether the rhythm is derived from dance steps (long, long, long, short, short, short or short, short, short, long), or the dance steps are derived from the additive rhythm (2 + 2 + 2 + 1 + 1 + 1 or 2 + 2 + 2 + 3). For other additive patterns, see "Chapter 21: Five and Ten," in this Section.

The following figure shows *danse orientale karshlamá,* a.k.a. 9/8. The grouping of the rhythmic pluses 2 + 2 + 2 + 1 + 1 + 1, are counted "ONE, two, ONE, two, ONE, two, ONE, TWO, THREE." The essential group sequence is 2 + 2 + 2 + 3.

accents:	>		>		>		>	>	>
beats:	1	2	3	4	5	6	7	8	9
drumtones:	D	•	T	•	D	•	T	T	T
pitch:	low		high		low		high	high	high
duration:	long		long		long		short	short	short

A variant of the *danse orientale karshlamá*, often used in alternation with it, is counted as "ONE, two, ONE, two, ONE, two, ONE, (two , three), with the second and third beats of the last cell (of three beats) silent. The essential group sequence is 2 + 2 + 2 + 3.

accents:	>		>		>		>		
beats:	1	2	3	4	5	6	7	8	9
drumtones:	D	•	T	•	D	•	T	•	•
pitch:	low		high		low		high		
duration:	short		short		short		long		

The next set of examples represent four *basic* regional versions: Turkish-Anatolian, Armenian, Greek, and Arabic. Each type is characterized in performance by localized preferences for tempo, variation, elaboration, and ornamentation styles. Modern *danse orientale 9/8* uses the Turkish-Anatolian version as its main model.

Turkish-Anatolian

accents:	>		>		>		>		
beats:	1	2	3	4	5	6	7	8	9
drumtones:	D	•	T	•	D	•	T	T	T

Armenian

accents:	>		>		>		>		
beats:	1	2	3	4	5	6	7	8	9
drumtones:	D	•	T	•	D	•	T	•	T

Greek

accents:	>		>		>		>		
beats:	1	2	3	4	5	6	7	8	9
drumtones:	D	•	T	•	D	•	T	T	•

Arabic

accents:	>		>		>		>		
beats:	1	2	3	4	5	6	7	8	9
drumtones:	D	•	T	•	D	•	T	•	•

Perhaps the most-recorded example of a Turkish *karshlamá* is the song "Rampi Rampi." Hear John Bilezikjian's Armenian-style version on his *Sirocco* CD (with Var Daghdevirian on drums) CD31001 Dantz Records, track #2 "Rompi, Rompi." For examples of Gypsy (Roma) Turkish and Anatolian styles, see *Masters of Turkish Music*, CD1051 Rounder Records, track #7; and also, Erköse Ensemble, *Tzigane: the Gypsy Music of Turkey*, CD3010 CMP Records, track #1b "Rumeli Karsilamasi." There are numerous Greek collections containing a *karsilamas* (*antikrystos*) dance or two. An Arabic night club example is found on Suhaila Salimpour's *Bal Anat, In The Beginning*, HMCD 98142, track #4 "Karshilama."

CHAPTER 19: PERSIAN SHISH-HASHT (6/8)

Iran is a diverse cultural complex whose strongest ethnic component is that of the prevailing Persian culture. Classical music is thought to have been synthesized during in the Qajar Period (1785–1925), combining earlier theory and practice, including instrument and technique influences from the Mongol invasions between 1200 to 1400 CE. The folk music of the Baluchi, Kordi, and Gilaki subcultures within Iran, among others, are also important elements. European orchestral and band influences (notation, harmony, counterpoint, and instruments) have been incorporated as well, beginning in the 1800s and continuing into the present within various popular music genres. Although Persian *shish-hasht* (six-eight) is not a typical rhythm used by the belly dance community, and is emphatically *not* used among Iranians for such purposes, increasing numbers of western dancers are using it as a vehicle for performance—in the expanded definition of *danse orientale* as inclusive of more than Arabic and Turkish music and dance.

Shish-hasht is the typical rhythm in Iranian popular music—especially that produced by diaspora immigrants and their decedents in southern California (among other places). The rhythm is sometimes referred to as *shir-e madar* ("milk of the mother")—inferring its importance to Persian cultural identity. While it is considered most "authentic" when realized on the *tombak* (see the sidebar on the next page), it can be played on the *dumbek* (a.k.a. Arabic *tabla*, etc.), western drumset, and electronically.

A compound duple meter in a cycle of six, it is divided into two groups: 3 + 3 with the strong duple pulse marked on the first

down-beat of each group of three—123, **456**. The rhythm is characterized (most importantly) by an emphasis (>) on beats 1, 3, 4, and 5, creating a quality sometimes referred to as *kereshmeh* ("lilt" or "flirt")—a kind of a swing feel. (Note that in Persian classical music this term also refers to a type of rhythmic and melodic structuring.) The following example illustrates a basic rendition, using *dumbek* notation, of the *shish-hasht* pattern without any embellishments. The Xs represent the duple pulse of the meter.

X			**X**		
>		>	>	>	
1	2	3	**4**	5	6
D	•	T	**D**	T	•

The resonant goblet-shaped *tombak* (18 inches x 10.5 inches) is the main Persian drum (see illustration). The drum is also known as the *zarb* (considered a colloquial name). It is manufactured on a lathe from a single aged trunk of hardwood: mulberry, walnut, and more recently *zaban gonjeshk*, a light-colored wood from a tree of the Sycamore family. Its interior tube and cylinder are sometimes partially chiseled out as well as lathed for the purpose of fine-tuning the instrument. The exterior surface is left either unadorned, incised with horizontal bands, or carved with historical bas-reliefs. It is then stained or left natural, and

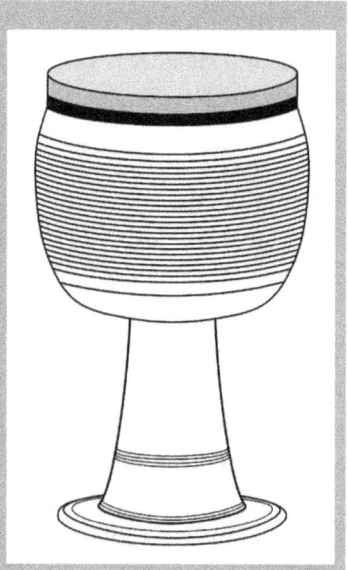

varnished. Some *tombaks* feature complex mosaic designs called *khatam* ("hammered")—laminated onto the surface with sheets of photographically treated plastic or created by an artist with individually placed pieces. Mass produced versions are made from softer woods such as pine. They are constructed of cut-out blocks that are glued together, and then lathed. Cow and camel calf, or traditional lamb provides the organic material of the drumhead—preferred because it is thicker than that of a goat (traditionally used for the Arabic *tabla*).

Persian *tombak* playing style is the most complex among the *dumbek* family of drums. The large diameter of the tombak drumhead allows for wide tonal manipulation. It is distinguished by the use of the resonant bass tone called *tom* (similar to *dum* on the *dumbek*), a treble drum-tone called *kenar bak* played on the edge with fingertips (similar to *tek* on the *dumbek*) or by a left-handed snapping technique called *palang* (leopard), and by the use of complex finger rolling ornaments (*takriz* and *taazin*), for example, the *meyaneh bak riz*, the *riz-e pour*, and the *eshareh* leading into *tom*.

Examples of music [with Persian 6/8] from Iran, and its diaspora, abound on the internet both for sale and as free sound clips. The website HTTP://WWW.KERESHMEH.COM is an important source for new and traditional *dastgâh* music (modal-based classical). Excellent sources for everything else Persian may be found at:

HTTP://WWW.CALTEXRECORDS.COM

CHAPTER 20: FLAVORS OF SEVEN

There are many flavors of rhythms in the cycle of seven found throughout Greece, Turkey, Iran, and the Arabic-speaking countries. Although asymmetrical compared to even-numbered cycles, seven-cycle rhythms are very danceable.

Like the asymmetrical Turkish karshlamá (or Greek karsilamas)—a popular rhythm among belly dancers grouped as 2 + 2 + 2 + 3 beats equaling a nine-beat cycle—the following examples of patterns in seven-beat cycles are grouped into sets of two- and three-beat cells. The most typical of these groupings are: 2 + 2 + 3 or 3 + 2 + 2. They can be thought of, in terms of dance gesture and steps, as short-short-long or long-short-short. Asymmetrical (odd-numbered cycles such as seven or nine) dance rhythms in the Mediterranean and Middle-Eastern regions tend to be played in sets of two cycles (7 + 7)—a question-and-answer form. The pairing creates an overall symmetrical form conducive to dance.

The Turkish rhythm *laz* represents the principle 2 + 2 + 3 version. The Iranian *haft zarbi*, the Arabic rhythms *nawakht* and *dwar Hindi*, and the Greek rhythm *kalamatiano* represent the more common 3 + 2 + 2 versions. It is important to remember that while the grouping of beat cells may be the same, the feel or style of realization varies between region and locality. In other words, there are many flavors!

Laz is associated with a historically mixed ethnic group which resides around the Turkish and Georgian coast of the Black Sea. Their traditional 2 + 2 + 3 rhythm is fast (used for line dancing) and has at least two variations, as depicted on the next page:

D • D • T • • or D T T T T T T

Another similarly named rhythm found in modern Egypt called *laz bar* (a.k.a. *Ali Pasha*) follows the 3 + 2 + 2 form:

D T T D T T T

The Iranian *haft* (seven) *zarbi* (beat) 3 + 2 + 2 rhythm emphasizes the lilting quality of the three—typical of the Persian style found in *shish hasht* (six-eight):

D • T D • T •

The Andalusian western Arabic *muwashah* 3 + 2 + 2 rhythm *nawakht* is found mostly in classical music, but versions of it show up in popular music. It has the stately tempo and feel typical of classical Arabic music rhythms. The core drum-tone sequence for it is:

D • T D • T T

Dwar Hindi (*dwar* indicating "cycle" or "turn"; also a 19TH-century vocal style sung in regional Arabic) is common to both the western and eastern Arabic classical music scene. The core drum-tone 3 + 2 + 2 sequence for it is:

D T T D • T •

Finally, perhaps the most relevant to belly dancing adaptations (like the *karshlamá*), is the 3 + 2 + 2 *kalamatiano*. By adaptation, it is meant that *karshlamá* and *kalamatiano* are not solo dances in their traditional context, but are often danced that way by belly dancers. It is associated with an ancient vigorous Greek folk rhythm and chain-dance called the *ormo*. One of the suggested origins of the name is that it comes from the folk-song "Kalamatiani"—a song genre about local girls from the town of Kalamata on the southwestern shore of the Peloponnesus.

While the Greek national dance *syrtos* (a dragging/pulling hand-holding line-dance) is also danced to a 2-beat cycle rhythm, depending upon what region (north or south) of Greece you're in, the *kalamatiano* rhythm is considered by some as the *syrtos* rhythm of choice in modern Greece.

The core drum-tone sequence for *kalamatiano* is **D T T D • T •**, and is often alternated as **D T T D • T • / D • T D • T •**. The question/answer (or call/response) form fits this the dance well. One typical way the *syrtos* dance is performed to *kalamatiano* is to cross three steps to the right (RLR) then two (LR) plus two (LR) in place, and then do the same again in the reverse direction (LRL + RL + RL).

If you listen to *kalamatiano* you can hear the shape of its long-short-short pattern. It is denoted on the downbeat of each cell by the drum-tones: *Dum* (3), *Dum* (2), *Tek* (2). The *Dum—Dum Tek* flow is a strong undercurrent in the rhythm, and is important to line dancers in feeling the music. The use of drum-tones in this way is common to most dance music of the Mediterranean and Middle East.

The notation on the next page shows the rhythms discussed in this article. Notice their similarities and differences. The style of the in-between rhythmic ornamentations of the basic pattern, like the interpretation of dance steps, is based upon local and regional taste. There are lots of flavors.

```
>              >              >
1    2    3    4    5    6    7
D    •    D    •    T    •    •
```
Laz 1

```
>              >              >
1    2    3    4    5    6    7
D    T    T    T    T    T    T
```
Laz 2

```
>                   >              >
1    2    3         4    5    6    7
D    T    T         D    T    T    T
```
Laz bar

```
>                   >              >
1    2    3    4    5    6    7
D    •    T    D    •    T    •
```
Haft zarbi

```
>                   >              >
1    2    3    4    5    6    7
D    •    T    D    •    T    T
```
Nawakht

```
>                   >              >
1    2    3    4    5    6    7
D    T    T    D    •    T    •
```
Dwar Hindi

```
>                   >              >
1    2    3    4    5    6    7
D    (T)  T    D    •    T    •
```
Kalamatiano

CHAPTER 21: FIVE AND TEN

Most dancers do not move outside of symmetrical standardized rhythmic cycles set in 2, 3, 4, 6, 8, 12, and 16 beats. So-called "odd" cycles such as 5, 7, 9, 10, 11, 13, etc., are overlooked, with the exception of the occasional nine-beat cycle rhythm called *karshlamá*. Belly dance rhythms in the time cycle of five or ten beats are uncommon in dance routines. Yet, patterns in odd cycles are inherently danceable, and can be arranged to be more symmetrical than one might think. The following article introduces and compares several rhythms set in the time cycles of five and ten.

The structure of rhythms set in odd-numbered time cycles, in this case five and ten, may be viewed in two ways. The first is to view the number of beats in a cycle like divisions in a pie. This view is typical to Western musical theory, and is called the *divisive system*—a circle can be divided into many portions equal or not, deriving (in part) from Greek math. The second way of viewing the structure of a rhythm is to create it out of pieces, making an additive form. The *additive system* is how the Arabic, Turkish, and Persian musical theorists define a rhythmic mode. This system is also related to the north and south Indian *tala* system.

In the additive system, *rhythmic modes* are constructed out of segments made out of equal pulses. Each segment, or cell, is categorized as being short (one or two pulses) or long (three pulses) in duration, and being heavy or light or strong or weak in intensity. The low-pitched *Dum* is considered heavy or strong (*thaqil*), and high-pitched *Tek*, which is considered light or weak (*khafif*). The origin of the rhythmic modes is drawn mostly from written and spoken texts (poetry).

The underlying structure (the mode) is retained in any realization (performance of the rhythm); the pattern of the long and short cells of a given mode remains the same at any size. For example, the rhythmic mode of *masmudi saghrir* is set in a cycle of eight beats, and is expressed as D D • T D • T •. Its variations—*baladi*, *maqsum*, *fellâhi*, *sa'idi*, and *fezzani*—are set in cycles of two or four, but still retain the proportional scale of the essential pattern of *Dums* (lows) and *Teks* (highs) that define the mode.

For the case of cycles of five and ten, one can see in the illustration below using the cells of 2 and 3, how there are a limited number of practical possibilities for the arrangement of short and long segments. However, the added element of light or heavy stress via the drum-tones *Tek* and *Dum*, allows for a wider variation of rhythm modes based upon the simple cellular groupings.

Five
3 + 2
2 + 3

Ten
3 + 3 + 2 + 2
2 + 2 + 3 + 3

3 + 2 + 3 + 2
2 + 3 + 2 + 3

3 + 2 + 2 + 3
2 + 3 + 3 + 2

In dance, counting the number of beats in a cycle tends to be less important than the *length* of the sonic gestures (melodies and rhythms) from which the dancer cues. *Accents* (points of stress louder than other notes or sounds before or after them) tend to be on the first note of a cell in the groupings of 2s and 3s. Thus, actually counting the beats in long rhythmic cycles, or odd cycle,

for a dancer becomes less important (once the rhythm is learned) than *feeling* the regular accents.

In the following illustration of rhythms below, note where the accents fall. Note also, the symmetrical arrangement of the cells in the cycles of ten: 3 + 2 + 2 + 3, for example. In performance, rhythms are often expressed in sets of two cycles so that a kind of question-and-answer phrase is created. This is accomplished in various ways. A common technique is to play the second iteration of the rhythm in a pairing quieter, or to alter some aspect of its pattern or tone. For example, replacing the drum-tone *Dum* with a *Tek* on the first note of the rhythm in the second iteration. D = Dum; T = Tek; K = Ka (left hand Tek); > = accent; • = rest (silence).

>		>						
1	2	3	4	5				
D	t k	D	T	t k				

koroglu—Turkish [2 + 3]

>		>						
1	2	3	4	5				
D	•	T	•	T				

usul aghar aksak or Turk aksak; a'raj—Arabic [2 + 3]

>			>		>		>	
1	2	3	4	5	6	7	8	9
D	•	•	T	•	D	D	T	•

wazn samai thaqil—Arabic classical [3 + 2 + 2 + 3]

>			>		>		>	
1	2	3	4	5	6	7	8	9
D	•	T	K	•	D	•	T	•

usul asksak semai—Turkish classical [3 + 2 + 2 + 3]

>			>			>		>
1	2	3	4	5	6	7	8	9
D	D	T	D	T	•	T	K	T

usul lenk fahte —Turkey [(3 + 3 + 2 + 2]

>		>		>			>	
1	2	3	4	5	6	7	8	9
D	T	D	T	D	T	T	D	T

usul cengi harbi —Turkey [2 + 2 + 3 + 3]

>   >   >   >

The final illustration is a simple proximity comparison of all the rhythms. Note the differences in drum-tones and accents (bold drum-tone letter) showing the long/short grouping.

	1	2	3	4	5	6	7	8	9	10
koroglu (2 + 3)	**D**	.	.	**D**	T					
a'raj (2 + 3)	**D**	.	T	T	.					
samai thaqil (3 + 2 + 2 + 3)	**D**	.	.	**T**	.	**D**	**D**	**T**	.	(T)
aksak semai (3 + 2 + 2 + 3)	**D**	.	T	**K**	.	**D**	.	**T**	.	T
jurjuna (3 + 2 + 2 + 3)	**D**	.	(T)	**T**	.	**D**	.	**T**	.	.
lenk fahte (3 + 3 + 2 + 2)	**D**	**D**	T	**D**	T	.	**T**	**K**	T	K
cengi harbi (2 + 2 + 3 + 3)	**D**	T	**D**	T	**D**	T	**T**	**D**	T	T

Although these rhythms are not that easy to find in common recordings, they are out there. Keep your ears open, keep actively listening to music and figure out the time cycle and how the rhythms move across it.

CHAPTER 22: JURJUNA: THE TEN-BEAT CYCLE

The Armenian ten-beat rhythm *jurjuna*, and dance of the same name, is in current use within the belly dance community among troupes who include folkloric line dance pieces in their repertoire. *Jurjuna* (pronounced JUR-juna with a French "j") is also written as *jurjina* (Arabic) or *çurçuna* (Turkish). Generally accepted as originating in Armenia, the rhythm is popular in Iraq, Turkey, and Egypt. (In Egypt, jurjuna is referred to as *samai'i tawashii*.)

In the first example below, *jurjuna* is displayed in its basic form. The important identifying "melody" drum-tones that define the rhythmic pattern are the first beats of each grouping of beats: 3 + 2 + 2 + 3. This grouping forms an accented sequence of Long-Short-Short-Long, identifiable by the alternating bass (Dum) and treble (Tek) drum-tone sequence of Low-High-Low-High. The treble drum-tones (on beats 4 and 8) are given more emphasis, inducing a kind of "swinging" motion, and echoing the same effect in rhythms such as *fellâhi* and *ayyub*.

As with all Middle-Eastern rhythms, the spaces between the rhythm melody are decorated with improvised elaborations and flourishes. In the second example, a few characteristic mid-tone fill strokes (*Ka*—left-hand stroke; *Tak*—right-hand stroke) have been added. The speed at which the beats flow is quick (150 bpm for a dotted quarter-note), but the accentual structure of the pattern (on beats 1, 4, 6, and 8) gives it the impression of being slower. An interesting side note: The arrangement of the grouping of the beats of the pattern make a palindrome: 3 2 2 3.

>			>		>		>		
1	2	3	4	5	6	7	8	9	10
D	•	•	T	•	D	•	T	•	•

>			>		>		>		
1	2	3	4	5	6	7	8	9	10
D	•	k	T	•	D	•	T	k	t

One of the best recorded examples of *jurjuna* comes from John Bilezikjian's *Armenian Connection* CD, Dantz Records, 2000. "Armenian Medley," track #8, consists of five songs strung together into a 9:44 minute piece—typical of music for line dances at parties. Dancers who wish to learn the dance that accompanies *jurjuna* should seek out the excellent instruction of Helen Bilezikjian, wife of famed musician/composer John Bilezikjian.

CHAPTER 23: ELEVEN

Rhythms set in a cycle of eleven beats are not common to standard belly dance. Yet, the cycle of eleven (a prime number) is a potential platform for dance movement in modern interpretive belly dance. There are several types of eleven-beat cycle rhythms ranging from Turkish, Arabic, Bulgarian, and Yemeni. As additive rhythms, they are formed of "short" and "long" beat segments. (Refer to "Chapter 21: Five and Ten" in this Section, for a discussion on additive rhythm.) These patterns can also be considered *aksak*-type rhythms (see "Chapter 18: Karshlamá" in this Section). Enter the door of eleven.

The patterns below are shown as core rhythmic modes. The principle *Dums* and *Teks* mark the pattern and provide the sound cue for the dancer to perceive and synchronize with the structure of the rhythmic mode. In practice, the drummer reinforces the rhythmic mode, adds ornamentation that enhances the mode, echoes the melodic rhythms, and rhythmically interacts with the dancers. The segments are denoted herein with brackets ([ ]) set around the beat numbers.

The Turkish rhythm *tek verus* is grouped as 2 + 3 + 2 + 2 + 2.

```
[1   2]   [3   4   5]   [6   7]   [8   9]   [10   11]
D    •    T    •   T    D    •    T    •    T     •
```

Arabic *awis* (Arabic, "difficult") is made of three segments: 3 + 4 + 4.

```
[1   2   3]   [4   5   6   7]   [8   9   10   11]
D   •    T    D   •   T   k     D   D   •    T
```

Another 11-beat cycle rhythm is found in western Bulgaria where odd-numbered rhythms used in folk dancing abound. It is used for a type of dance called *kopanitsa* or *gankino*. The name derives from the "digging" or "hoeing" (Bulgarian—*kopam*) motions used in the dance, corresponding with the "three" segment in the additive sequence 2 + 2 + 3 + 2 + 2 that makes up this rhythm. The following illustration shows two renditions (*a* and *b*) of the Bulgarian *kopanitsa* as translated to the *dumbek*:

	[1	2]	[3	4]	[5	6	7]	[8	9]	[10	11]
a)	D	•	T	•	D	t	k	T	•	T	•
b)	D	•	T	•	D	•	T	D	•	T	•

In Macedonia, the *neda voda* rhythm is grouped 2 + 2 + 2 + 2 + 3, and translated to *dumbek* as:

[1	2]	[3	4]	[5	6]	[7	8]	[9	10	11]
D	t k	T	t k	D	t k	T	t k	D	D	•

The Yemeni classical 11-beat cycle rhythm, grouped as 2 + 3 + 3 + 3 is called *das'a kabir*, and translates to the *dumbek* as:

[1	2]	[3	4	5]	[6	7	8]	[9	10	11]
D	•	T	•	•	T	•	•	T	•	•

In comparing the rhythms illustrated above, at least two aspects can be noted:

1. Rhythms placed in the 11-beat cycle are additive. That is, they consist of sequences of short (2) or long (3, 4 or 5) groups of beats.

2. The rhythm, no matter what arrangement of short and long segments, forms an asymmetrical pattern with one exception: *kopanitsa*. Note that the segment arrangement of *kopanitsa* is symmetrical like that of the 10-beat cycle

rhythm known as *jurjuna*: 3 + 2 + 2 + 3. Other possibilities (not illustrated herein) include segment arrangements of 3 + 3 + 2 + 3 and 4 + 4 + 3.

The following number sets compares the groupings noted in the above illustrations:

tek verus	2 + 3 + 2 + 2 + 2
awis	3 + 4 + 4
kopanitsa	2 + 2 + 3 + 2 + 2
neda voda	2 + 2 + 2 + 2 + 3
das'a kabir	2 + 3 + 3 + 3

These patterns may seem formidable to dance to, but they are not. Like all asymmetrical patterns, those in eleven need not be difficult to understand if one senses the segment durations as short and long. These durations translate easily into motion. Regarding segment duration as "short" or "long" is common practice among musicians, and among dancers in the cultures from which these rhythms derive. However, counting cycle beats is a fundamental skill all dancers should cultivate in addition to *feeling* the rhythms.

As practice to understand this concept try the following exercise: Using a sequence of 2 + 2 + 3 + 2 + 2, clap your hands on the first down-beat of each segment. Make a strong accent on the first down-beat of the entire pattern to mark that it is the principle "One" in the cycle. As you clap recite: "ONE, two, One, two, One, two, three, One, two, One, two." Next, while continuing to clap and maintaining the eleven-beat pulse of the cycle, switch to saying "short" (for two beats) and "long" (for three beats). See next page.

beat:	1	2	3	4	5	6	7	8	9	10	11
clap:	X		X		X			X		X	
say:	1	2	1	2	1	2	3	1	2	1	2
say:	short		short		long			short		short	

How does something asymmetrical become symmetrical? As with any odd-numbered asymmetrical pattern, eleven feels syncopated and irregular until it is phrased as a pair: 11 + 11. Pairing is the common method of phrasing rhythmic patterns and melodies in order to create symmetry. A customary phrase-pairing method is the so-called *Question-and-Answer* (a.k.a. *Call-and-Response*) form. The *Question* states the rhythm as is without alteration. The *Answer* portion of the pair is altered in some way. Changing the first drum-tone of a sequence, for example, by replacing a *Dum* with a *Tek*, is a typical method. The following illustration shows one possible solution with this Q/A arrangement using the *kopanitsa b* rhythm (see above). The variation of the drum-tone is marked by **bolding**. Notice how the alternation of the *Dum* and *Tek* on the first down-beat creates an interesting twist to the *aksak* syncopation of the pattern.

Another important aspect shown in the following example is how symmetry is achieved in pairing through the alternation of the direction of motion by the dancer. Beneath the drum-tones in the notation, one possible solution of alternating direction of motion (step, gesture, position) for a dancer is given. The changes occur at the beginning of each segment (shown as R for right and L for left). Hence, on the first iteration the right foot leads, and on the second iteration the left foot leads.

Question											Answer										

	1	2	3	4	5	6	7	8	9	10	11	1	2	3	4	5	6	7	8	9	10	11	
‖:	**D**	•	T	•	D	•	T	D	•	T	•	**T**	•	T	•	D	•	T	D	•	T	•	:‖
	R		L		R			L		R		L		R				L	R		L		

Studying complex, irregular rhythms will open the door to a new universe of interesting potentials for modern interpretive belly dance. Although not a "standard" rhythm for cabaret and other *danse orientale* forms, rhythms in eleven and other odd-numbered cycles can be an exciting change. Ask your local musicians to play something in eleven!

Belly Dance Rhythm Resource

SECTION IV
SPECIALIZED RHYTHMS:
ETHNIC & FOLK DANCE

North Africa, East Africa, and The Mid-East—
The Major Countries of Origin or Influence of Belly Dance Music

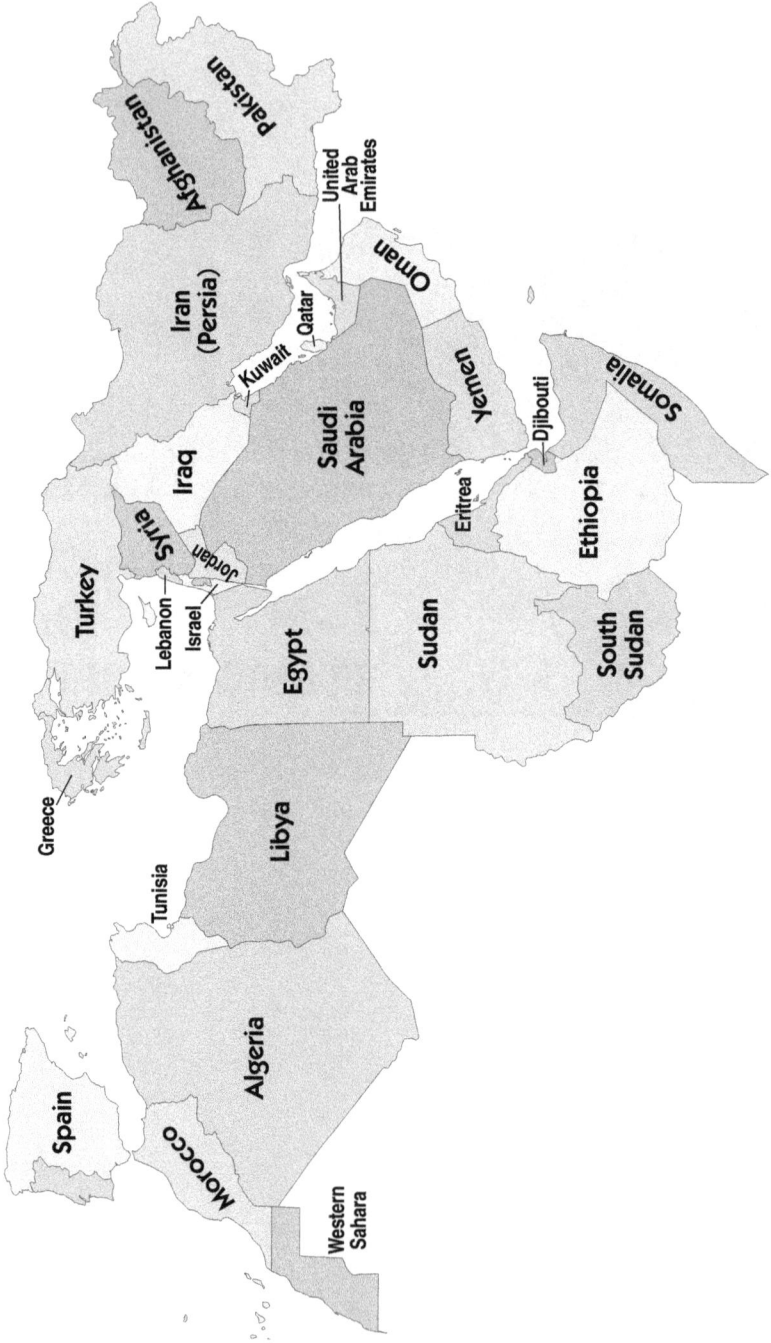

CHAPTER 24: DANSE ZAR—THE FASCINATING RHYTHM

The word *zar* is a variant of the Arabic word *zahar* ("he visited") or *zahr* ("he became visible, perceptible, or manifest"). Traditional *zar* (pronounced z-ah-r) is a communal healing ritual combining trance-inducing sound (drumming, clapping, singing), rhythmic breathing, and movement led by a shamaness called a *kodia* or *sheikha*. *Zar* "music" is a complex rhythmic field made with drumming, percussion, and clapping. There are also male-led *zar* ceremonies. The purpose of the *zar* ritual is to heal an afflicted subject by the appeasement and removal of malevolent *zayran*—male *jinn*, astral spirit-beings capable of interacting with humans. Psychic illness, in the context of the cultural belief that supports *zar* ritual, is linked to physical illness, and general disease in the wider sense. Zar is not an exorcism in the Xtian sense, however, but is rather a method (ritual) in which a balance is restored resulting in health and well-being.

Traditional *zar* ceremonies are found in southern Egyptian villages, northern Sudan, Ethiopia, and Somalia. These events occur in homes (backyards) or in public communal spaces, depending upon who has paid for the ritual to be performed. Similar folk ceremonies under different names and varying contexts are found throughout southern Iran, the Levant, and the Maghreb. Disparaged as superstitious and antiquated, conservative Muslims tolerate *zar* rituals as a cathartic activity for villagers. It is viewed by its practitioners as a powerful, cleansing, and balancing event crucial to psychical/physical well being.

In modern times, exhibitions of *zar* (or aspects of it) are "danced" on stage for audiences who pay to come and sit quietly in a chair, in front and below a lit proscenium stage,

and watch. This context is abstracted from the traditional folk setting. During a traditional *zar* ceremony, the progression of events is not as linear as a staged show. Although the arc of the event begins with a "drawing-in" segment, and then slowly moves into more and more powerful levels of engagement, an intense catharsis, and a final release and return, un-staged folk realizations of these gatherings are far more chaotic, starting and stopping and evolving within the conditions of the moment. The participants (friends of the afflicted, musicians, observers) are not an audience in the western sense. They are integral to the ritual, lending their support through participation in the music (clapping, responsorial singing, percussion), and focusing their intent upon the afflicted being healed.

Egyptian dance artist Nadia Gamal was among the first professional performers (in 5-star nightclubs in Cairo) to extract aspects of *zar* ritual (rhythm and dance movement), and incorporate them into a segment within a staged dance suite (c. 1968). Some of the movements (hair tossing, whirling, and swaying in place) derived from *zar* are also present in the dancing actions for Persian Gulf music such as the *khalīji* family. (See "Chapter 27: Khalīji" in this Section) Therefore, during a staged performance, those actions must be contextualized (made apparent they are "zar," and not another kind of dance) for the audience by the method of presentation through image as "ritualistic," and by the dancer(s) acting out the progression of the ritual. There is no popular broadcast *zar* music, and it has so far not been converted into a musical commodity, as have other folk music styles. In staged settings, the percussion section of the house ensemble plays a mock version of "typical" *zar* ritual rhythmic music. It is usually a set piece, and has little variation compared to the fluxing rhythms of a traditional rendition.

For traditional ceremonies, specialized, experienced, musicians (who work as *zar* musicians) are hired. The *sheikha* gives the musicians (and participants) cues through her voice and with her frame drum. She senses and plays the appropriate "thread" rhythm for the *zayran* (there may be more than one) in the afflicted person. Evolving through the course of the ritual, the shifting "thread" rhythm is interpreted and reacted to, by the musicians. This type of non-static heterophonic improvisation (driven by loops of learned rhythm modules, i.e., the "thread") creates a distracting rhythmic field with which the *sheikha* leads the subject into a hypnotic-like state. As the *sheikha's* voice rises above and entwines the shifting polyrhythms, she interacts on both literal and mental levels. Several dance ethnologists have written about the details of the process and meaning of *zar* ritual. See suggested list at the end of this chapter.

The basic instruments of a *zar* ritual are simple drums (frames, the Arabic *tabla*, the *riq*) and percussion (hand-clapping, household items, pots and pans, washtubs), and the voice. A tall brass mortar called the *tisht* (Sudan) is used in some instances. The kinds of drums, percussion, and melody instruments vary from locale to locale, and are somewhat irrelevant. Only the frame drum may be said to have significance as a historic instrument of the shaman(ess). It is the rhythmic "thread," as expressed by the *sheikha* that has the deepest level of symbolic importance. The "thread" rhythm and its expression (relevant to the moment) can be created on any drum or percussive object.

One rhythm has been abstracted from *zar*, however, by Egyptian musicians playing for dancers in stage performances in the *cabaret* context. Staged folkloric exhibitions (on university stages, or at dance festivals) also use this rhythm. It functions as the "zar rhythm," and is herein called *danse zar*. This is the rhythm

taught by belly dance instructors, and is in wide use. The *danse zar* pattern is identical to *ayyub* (refer to "Chapter 13: Ayyub" in Section II, "Chapter 9: A Rhythmic Guide" in Section I, and "Chapter 28: Karachi" in this Section).

1	e	&	> a	**2**	e	> &	a
X				X			
D	•	•	T	D	•	T	•

The *danse zar* pattern is played at a slow tempo at around 80± bpm, compared to the much faster-tempo *ayyub,* played at around 126± bpm. The slow tempo gives the rhythm a strong, driving, heavy, in-ward inducing quality, compared to the lighter more strident and active out-ward quality of *ayyub.*

A principle sonic characteristic of *danse zar* (as it is realized on the Arabic *tabla* or frame drum) is the apparent audible separation of the drum-stroke tone of low-pitched *Dum* and high-pitched *Tek*—as if they were on two different time levels. The strident emphasis of the low-pitched *Dums* creates a solid ground over which the high-pitched *Teks* seem to float. Alternation of the syncopated pattern, D • • T, with the regular pattern, D • T •, is key to motion induction. Otherwise D • • T is only a skipping figure, and D • T • only a simple low-high alternation. Both these aspects of *danse zar* reflect spiritual analogs.

For more detail and discussion on this fascinating rhythm and dance in its traditional and adapted forms, see resources on the following page.

Audio-Visual

Aisha Ali's video "Dances of Egypt" (Araf Video, 1991)—includes a short segment of the *Masri Zar Ensemble* and dancers filmed by Laurie Eisler with slides by Becky Stone.

Anthropo-Ethnological Writings

Janice Boddy, *Wombs and Alien Spirits: Women, Men, and the Zar Cult in Northern Sudan*, Madison: The University of Wisconsin Press, 1989.

Hani Fakhouri, "Zar Cult in an Egyptian Village," *Anthropological Quarterly* 41.1: 1968, 49–56.

Tahgi Modarressi, "The Zar Cult in Southern Iran," *Trance and Possession States*, edited by Raymond Prince, Montreal: R.M. Bucke Memorial Society, 1968, 149–55.

Magda Saleh, "Dance in Egypt," *The Garland Encyclopedia of World Music*, vol. 6, "The Middle East," edited by Virginia Danielson, Scott Marcus, and Dwight Reynolds. New York: Routledge, 2002, 632–633.

For a Wider Perspective, See

Mircea Eliade, *Shamanism: Archaic Techniques of Ecstasy*, Princeton, New Jersey: Princeton University Press, 1972.

Marguerite Kusuhara (with Richard Adrian Steiger), "Ethnography of an Epiphany: Physiological/Psychological Indications for Trance-like Behaviors in Middle-Eastern Dance," *Habibi Journal*, vol. 19.2, Santa Barbara: Habibi Publications, 2002, 56–61. Now online at HTTP://THEBESTOFHABIBI.COM/TABLEOFCONTENTS/

Online Resources (Articles, Photos, Music, Movies)

"Zar Ceremony" by Heba Fatteen Bizzari at HTTP://WWW.TOUREGYPT.NET/FEATURESTORIES/ZAR.HTM

"The Zar-Trance Music for Women" (Sands of Time Music CD) at HTTP://WWW.SERPENTINE.ORG/SoT/SoToo1ZAR.HTM

"Beat Mania" (author unknown), Al-Ahram Weekly Online, 9–15, November 2006, issue No. 819 at HTTP://WEEKLY.AHRAM.ORG.EG/2006/819/FE2.HTM

Downloadable PDF by Me'ira (Karol Harding) titled "The Zar Revisited" at HTTP://WWW.DANCEGYPT.COM/FILES/ZAR.PDF

CHAPTER 25: FELLÂHI

The *fellâhi* (pronounced, feh-LAH-hee) rhythm is the most common traditional rhythm among the fellahîn culture. The word *fellahîn* comes from the Arabic verb *falaha,* to "cultivate." It also is defined as "ploughman," or "tiller." Whatever the exact shade of meaning taken from the word, it is used as a general term for the indigenous rural agriculturalists who live by the Nile and in the Delta. Many rural fellahîn live in mud-brick houses and till their soil in nearly the same way their ancestors did in the time of the Pharaohs. In modern times, some fellahîn have migrated into cities. The fellahîn are thought to represent around 60% of Egypt's population (circa 2000).

The *fellâhi* rhythm has the same core drum-note pattern as *maqsum* (DT •T D• T•), but is played within a time-cycle of two beats instead of four beats. This kind of compacting of a rhythm into a small space at twice the original speed is called "double-time" in western terminology. Notice that in the notation shown below, two lines underline the drum-note symbols—this indicates that four pulses fit in the space of the beat (1 e & a, 2 e & a).

To learn this rhythm (and thus be able to recognize it when you hear it), recite the *maqsum* rhythm, but clap the beat with two beats instead of four.

1	e	&	> a	**2**	e	&	> a
X				X			
D	T	•	T	D	•	T	•

Fellâhi is played at a fast tempo of around 120 bpm. The sonic result of the fast tempo places the *Dum*s close together in time. Note that the second and fifth drum-notes in the sequence are played louder than the rest of the drum-notes (the symbol > is a loudness accent). The enhanced repetitive and strident quality of the *Dum*s provide a foundation over which the high pitched, accented, *Tek* drum-notes seem to float.

Fellâhi is used to accompany traditional fellahîn village folkdances (the source of numerous movement elements that have been incorporated into belly dance). An excellent resource for these dances are the audio/visual field-recordings made by Aisha Ali (see her website HTTP://WWW.AISHA-ALI.COM). It is important to keep in mind that the *fellâhi* rhythm in modern belly dance music is not used all the way through a piece of music—*fellâhi* often serves as a double-time alternate for *maqsum* (for example) during vigorous dance segments. There are exceptions, however, such as its use in theatrical folkdance recreations. Examples of songs likely to have *fellâhi* in it are "Banat Iskandaria," and in the last fast section of compact dance suites such as "Eftetah Nahawand" and "Tamer Henna."

CHAPTER 26: FEZZANI AND FELLÂHI

Fezzani (Feh-ZAHN-ee) is a neglected rhythm in belly dance. Another permutation of the *masmudi* family), *fezanni* is a valuable alternate variation of *fellahīn* (see "Chapter 15: Masmudi—The Mother Rhythm" and "Chapter 16: Masmudi's Influence" in Section II) As discussed and illustrated in the aforementioned articles, the *fellâhi* rhythm (D T • T D • T • = two-beat cycle) is a derivative of *maqsum* (D T • T D • T • = four-beat cycle), both of which are generated from the eight-beat cycle "mother" rhythm *masmudi kabir* (D D • T • D • T). In this article, *fezzani* is compared with *fellâhi*.

The *fezzani* rhythm is thought to have originated in the Fezzan region of Libya (in the lower left quadrant bordered by the Sahara Desert and Nigeria below, and Algeria to the west), hence the eponymous name. In current use, *fezzani* is one of several rhythms used for the staged *Raqs al Juzur* (a.k.a. *Raqs Sharbia*), or the "jar dance," a national folk dance in Tunisia (on the Mediterranean coast between Algeria and Libya). Women use the jar as a prop, balancing it upon their heads while doing sharp horizontal hip twists, or moving the jar around with the hands in various simple to complex motions. A characteristic element of this dance is the progressive increase in tempo of the music, showing the skill of the dancer at balancing the jar. In some versions of this dance, male dancers also participate, with stylized flirtations, trying to distract the women into dropping the jar. There are many social overtones embedded in *Raqs al Juzur*.

It is possible that since *fezzani* came from the same general geographical area (north-western Africa) where *masmudi kabir* also originated, they are historically related. *Masmudi kabir* is

believed to have derived from a folk rhythm found among the *Masmuda*, an ancient tribal confederacy of agricultural Berbers living in the western part of north Africa. Western Arab court musicians in 13TH century Morocco and Tunisia first adapted the rhythm to the Arabic classical vocal suite called the *muwashahat* (Arabic for "girdled"). This may explain why the *fezzani* drum-tone pattern is so similar to *fellâhi*.

To learn *fezzani,* begin first by clapping a two-beat time cycle, and reciting the *fellâhi* rhythm as shown in the illustration below. *Fellâhi* is set in two beats, each of which is subdivided by four pulses, counted as 1 e & a, 2 e & a.

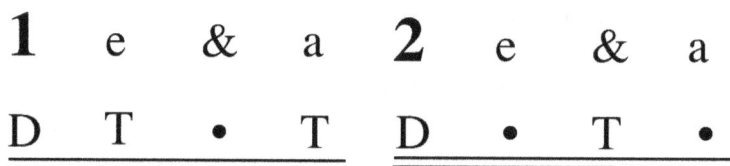

1	e	&	a	**2**	e	&	a
D	T	•	T	D	•	T	•

Fellâhi rhythm

As noted above, the principle difference between *fellâhi* and *fezzani* is how the pulses between the beats of the cycle are placed. Counting the time for *fellâhi* and *fezzani* is not tricky, but it does require an understanding of how musical rhythm can be shifted from a "two" to a "three" feel. It is not complicated.

In the following diagram, the inner pulse of the down-beats of the time cycle are shifted from a subdivision of four counted as 1 ee & ah 2 ee & ah, to a subdivision of six, counted as 1 ta ti & ta ti. The counting of subdivisions is for learning and teaching purposes, hence the actual words that are used are somewhat arbitrary. In western music the words used here are typical, but you may choose whatever words you want as place keepers. The main idea is that you feel the *three* pulse on the down-beat (the "one") and on the up-beat (the "and"): 1 2 3 1 2 3 (see illustration,

below). At first, clap the beat slowly and recite the threes until you have it in control, then increase the tempo. At this point, discard the place-keeping word, and count silently, feeling the pulses flow to the beat. *Fellâhi* and *fezzani* are both played quickly at a tempo of around 120± bpm (see the tempi table in "Chapter 34: Relationships—Masmudi" in Section V).

1	&	2	&
1 ta ti	**& ta ti**	**2 ta ti**	**& ta ti**
3	3	3	3

Fezzani rhythm in colloquial-word notation

Once you have a feel for how the threes fit in relationship to the beats of the cycle, try reciting the *fezzani* pattern, below, while continuing to clap. Remember that the symbol • in the notation represents a silent space (no sound). (D = Dum, T = Tek, k = ka). *Ka* replaces the *Teks* of *fellâhi* except the final note. The third *ka* (circled in the notation) in the *fezzani* sequence is optional. That is, it can be left out or added at the player's discretion. The drum-tone *ka* is a secondary drum-tone (slightly lower in pitch) to the principle *Tek* drum-tone, and is played with less force and farther into the drumhead. *Ka* is softer in quality (attack) than the harder, brighter, sounding *Tek*. The addition of *ka* is an attribute of the rolling feel, characteristic of some folk and classical styles of music in the Tunisian and Libyan musical realms.

1	**&**	**2**	**&**
D • k	**• • k**	**D •(k)**	**T • •**
3	3	3	3

Fezzani rhythm

Now that you have mastered the *fezzani* rhythm, take the next step. It is a bit more difficult, but once you get it, you will enjoy the ability (skill) to switch back and forth. This aspect, the alteration of the inner pulse between beats from a two (2, 4, 8) to a three (3 or 6) subdivision, is a feature of Indian music, and is important in Africa and Latin music.

The following diagram illustrates the shift from *fellâhi* to *fezzani*:

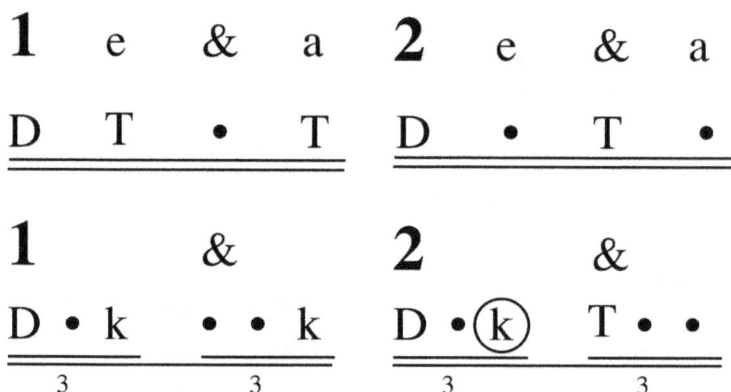

1	e	**&**	a	**2**	e	**&**	a
D	T	•	T	D	•	T	•

1		**&**		**2**		**&**	
D	• k		• • k	D	• (k)	T •	•

| 3 | 3 | 3 | 3 |

Fellâhi and Fezzani rhythm comparison

As an alternate to *fellâhi*, *fezzani* provides an interesting "twist." If you are a percussionist try to play it (using RLL RLR handing); you may enjoy it. If you are a dancer, request it the next time you dance to live music.

CHAPTER 27: KHALÎJI

Khalîji (khuh-LEE-jee) is both a dance and musical style found in the Arabic countries bordering the *Khalîj* (a.k.a. the Persian Gulf): Saudi Arabia, Iraq, Kuwait, Bahrain, Qatar, Oman, the United Arab Emirates (UAE), and Yemen. *Khalîj* is the singular noun for "gulf." The addition of the prefix "*al*" or the suffix "*i*" makes the term genitive, meaning from, or belonging to, the Gulf: *al Khalîj* or *khalîji*.

There are many varieties of the *khalîji* dance in the Gulf region, each with its own local name, costume, style, and rhythm (e.g., *raks naʿashat*, "girl's dance"). Overall, gliding and limping steps, hair tossing, and hand movements characterize *khalîji* dance. As part of the dance, dancers grasp and flourish the folds of the *thobe nashaʿar* or *nashal* (a traditional loose-fitting decorated costume dress. The gestures and actions of Gulf pearl divers are thought to be a generative source. Hair tossing, for example, may be reminiscent of the motion of ocean waves. While *khalîji* dance action can be theoretically derived from, and reflect, these kinds of processes, in its present form *khalîji* is abstracted from such origins. Modern and traditional *khalîji* music and dance is promulgated via technologies such as the internet, video, television, radio, and audio recordings (MP3s, CDs, cassettes, LPs).

The women's form of *khalîji* is only performed in private by women *for* women (at weddings, birthdays, etc.) due to restrictive religious Islamic Shariʿa laws in Saudi Arabia and other Gulf regions—women and men are segregated socially. There are exceptions to the rule, however, such as demonstrations at events such as the annual *Janadriya Heritage Festival* near

Riyâdh in Saudi Arabia during the *Women's Days*. The music is provided either by women musicians, or by recordings. Even though there is obvious segregation, at great public events like this festival, men are present as audience and behind the scenes (audio, stage, etc.). The influence of oil wealth has produced an Ameri-Europeanized urban upper class. In the context of disco-nightclubs in places such as Dubai, men and women dance *khalîji* in a non-genderized form together—emphasizing head movements, shoulder shimmies, limping or dipping steps, and upraised arms. Women dancers and dance groups from Arabic countries performing in Europe, the United States, and other western cultures, are able to freely perform modern and folkloric forms of *khalîji* in public.

Like the dance, the rhythm called *khalîji* may be derived from traditional sources. The "standard" *khalîji* rhythm (herein discussed) known to the *danse orientale* community, is considered to originate from the Yemeni rhythm called *adani* from Port Aden and the nearby region, and to a lesser extent *dawsarî* (after the Arabian bedouin tribe of the same name). *Adani*-based *khalîji* has become popularized in modern Gulf Arabic urban music in a similar way as the Egyptian *sai'di* rhythm (refer to "Chapter 12: Sa'idi" in Section II, as well as the analysis chapter "Chapter 34: Relationships—Masmudi" in Section V).

Associated with Saudi Arabia through its popular music industry, *khalîji* is sometimes called *Saudi*. Other more localized *khalîji* rhythms are *na'ashat* (UAE), and *samri* and *naggazi* (Kuwait). *Naggazi* is rhythmically similar to a Gulf musical style from Iran called *bandari* ("from the port")—a 6/8 pattern. Note that Persians use the term *khalîji* to refer to *bandari* as well as the other Arabic types discussed herein (see "Chapter 33: Shish-Hasht and Bandari" in Section IV). These rhythms (and their

dance motions) reflect the historical influences and interactions between Persians, East Indians, Black Africans, and Arabs—all cultures brought together by the commonality of the Gulf.

The standard popular *khalîji* rhythm is structured in the same way as *malfuf* (refer to "Chapter 14: Malfuf" in Section II). Although it is set in an even-numbered four-beat time cycle (subdivided into eight segments), the internal arrangement of the beats is asymmetrical: 3 + 3 + 2 = 8. Note that the version illustrated below is for solo drum. In practice, *khalîji* is often played on several drums in a polyrhythmic manner, the parts interlocking.

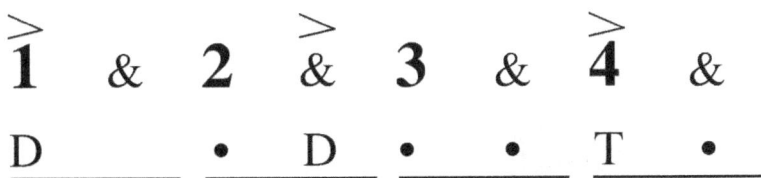

$\overset{>}{1}$	&	$\overset{>}{2}$	&	3	&	$\overset{>}{4}$	&
D		•	D	•	•	T	•

Khalîji is performed on the drum (*dumbek* or *tabla arabi*) in a less ornate manner compared to other popular rhythms like *baladi*, *maqsum*, *fellâhi*, and *malfuf*. Strong emphasis is placed upon the drum-note melody (*Dum Dum Tek*) creating a "heavy" trance-like syncopated feel. Although performed typically at a slow (90± bpm) tempo, it may be played faster or slower as necessary. Like most rhythms of the Middle East, the tempo of *khalîji* is adjusted to emphasize the emotional state being conveyed. At an even slower tempo (75± bpm), the *khalîji* rhythm becomes one of many *zar* healing rhythm "threads." (See "Chapter 24: Danse Zar—The Fascinating Rhythm" in this Section.)

To familiarize yourself with the varieties of *khalîji*, explore some suggestions for listening, on the next page.

Music from Yemen Arabia: Sanaani, Laheji, Adeni, CDROUN5156, Rounder Records, 1999.

Saudi Arabian popular *khalīji* is represented by Mohammed Abdo's *Al 'Amaken.*

Nourhan Sharif's *Arabic Rhythms,* CD, vol. 1, Egyptian Academy of Dance, track #7

Issam Houshan's The *Dancing Drum,* CD, track #17 are excellent renditions of the standard *khalīji* used in belly dance.

CHAPTER 28: KARACHI

Although not all that common in popular belly dance music, the two-beat cycle rhythm known as *karachi* (kah-RAH-tshee) sometimes spelled *karatchi*, is a useful and unique alternative to other two-beat patterns such as *ayyub* (refer to "Chapter 13: Ayyub" in Section II). Abstracted to pure rhythm without the drum-tones (*Dum* and *Tek*) that characterize any pattern, *karachi* is identical to *ayyub* and its slower version called *zar* (see Chapter 24: Danse Zar—The Fascinating Rhythm" in this Section). The following example shows the abstracted pattern. The symbol "o" above the double-line demarcates the rhythmic points; the letters D = *Dum*; T = *Tek*) below the double-line shows the *ayyub/zar* rhythm:

x				x			
1	e	&	a	2	e	&	a
o	•	•	o	o	•	o	•
D			T	D		T	

Compare the above to the following example of basic *karachi*:

x				x			
1	e	&	a	2	e	&	a
T	•	•	T	T	•	D	•

The principle characteristic of *karachi* is that the *Dum* is on the "and" of beat two. An example of classic syncopation, the *Dum* is

displaced to an unexpected position on an upbeat rather than a downbeat. This kind of shift of the position of the *Dum* is unique in Arabic belly dance rhythm, indicating it is not indigenous. Thus, while *karachi* is rhythmically identical to the *ayyub/zar* rhythm, the drum-tone positions make it quite different in feel. Both *karachi* and *ayyub* are, however, played at a fast tempo.

Where did this rhythm come from? The name suggests that it is from Pakistan; the name is the same as Pakistan's capital city Karachi. A closer look at the rhythm shows that it is similar to *chaal*, the basic pattern used for *bhangra* (a popular dance rhythm in Pakistan and India). As written in the spoken drum-tone words called *bols* used by *dhol* (a barrel-type drum) drummers in that region, the sequence for the basic *chaal-bhangra* rhythm is *Dha-na na-na na-dha dha-na*. *Dha* is the low-pitched and the high-pitched tone *na* together; *na* is the high-pitched tone alone. In the following illustration it can be seen that the final *dha* is in the same position as the *karachi Dum*. Note the *chaal* pattern is in triplets (an artificial grouping of three beats) and doesn't quite match the sixteenth-notes—optical match herein for the purpose of illustration.

X				X			
1	e	&	a	2	e	&	a
T	•	•	k	T	•	D	•
Dha - na		na - na		na - dha		dha – na	
3		3		3		3	

Although there is a concordance with the *Dum* and *dha*, the overall quality of *chaal-bhangra* is quiet different from *karachi*. *Bhangra* swings (is played "skippy"; in the illustration shown as triplets) while *karachi* is played flat without any swinging quality.

Whether there is a historical relationship is questionable, but nonetheless there is some similarity.

Another possible derivation of *karachi* is the *guaracha* pattern from Latin music. Brought to the New World via Spanish Iberia, one may speculate that the *guaracha* is an Arabic-influenced or -derived pattern like the *boléro* (see "Chapter 32: Boléro" in this Section). The *guaracha* is similar to *karachi* in two ways. First, the two names *karachi* and *guaracha* suggest a possible vowel or consonant shift due to language and pronunciation differences. Second, the low-pitched tone in *guaracha* is placed on the "and" of down-beat two as in *karachi*. These two similarities suggest some possible connection. The following example illustrates a basic interpretation of the *guaracha* rhythm:

Another possibility comes from a typical simple counter-rhythm, shown in the next illustration below, used with Cuban *rumba* and *calypso* which is also similar—the accent usually played as a low-pitched tone also on the "and" of the down-beat two as in *karachi*.

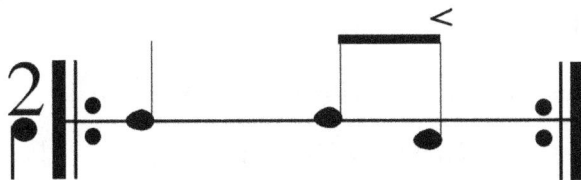

The infusion of Latin rhythm and percussion instruments into Arabic music presents an interesting puzzle. It is possible that

karachi is an interpretation of *guaracha* or *rumba*-like patterns like the Arabic *boléro*. With the vast circulation of people, materials, and cultural elements from Africa and Arabic cultures to the New World and back, and the recycling of instruments and rhythms, misunderstanding and mispronunciation of words are bound to happen. Distance, time, and culture may well have led to confusion and hybridization. The true origin of the *karachi* rhythm is therefore lost. *Karachi* is in widespread use throughout Egyptian and North African music. Its typical use in belly dance routines, in addition to being the solo pattern used throughout a piece, is as an inserted transitional pattern for entrances and endings in dance routines. Remember that the patterns on the previous page are basic versions. All patterns are decorated with a filigree of extra drum-tones in order to bring out their character.

Some musical examples of the wide varieties of the *karachi* rhythm can be found here:

Yallah Ya Helwa, "Ya Musafer," Yallah Dance, Inc.

Hossein Ramzy, *Rhythms of the Nile,* "Karachi"

Mahmoud Fadl, *Drummers of the Nile*, "South Nubian and Sudanese Rhythms: Karachi" [Note: this one sounds like the *guaracha* type]

Chalf Hassan, *Songs and Dances from Morocco*," Lahssab, Talata We-Talatin"

Issam Houshan's, *The Dancing Drum*, "Karatchi"

Helm, *Itneen—Tribal Dance/Tribal Drums*, "Karachi Unplugged," and "Karachi Cruisin'"

Various Artists, *Visit Me In Bahgdad*, Abart Al Shat "Crossing the Coast"

CHAPTER 29: CHOBIYYAH AND BAMBI

Chobiyyah (cho-BEE-yah) is an infectious rhythm used for an Iraqi line dance (of the same name) similar to the Lebansese *debke*, but specific to Iraq instead of Lebanon. *Chobiyyah* is sometimes foreshortened to *chobi* or *chobie* in common spoken usage. The *chobiyyah* dance, like *debke*, has a leader who winds his way around the dance space followed by a hand- or shoulder-holding line. Like *debke*, it is also popular at weddings and other social gatherings (refer to "Chapter 31: Debke" in this Section). Although *chobiyyah* is not a belly dance rhythm *per se*, it can easily be adapted into folk-based routines, as have many other patterns.

The following notation illustrates a four-beat (a) and a six-beat (b) version. Note that four-beat *chobiyyah* has the two-beat *malfuf* pattern (3 + 3 + 2; D•• T•• T•) in the second half on beats 3 and 4. (See "Chapter 14: Malfuf" in Section II.) The six-beat version of *chobiyyah* adds another iteration of *malfuf* on beats 5 and 6. Note also, that the last two down-beats (3 and 4 in the first example, and 5 and 6 in the second example) are used to support the two heavy steps (stomp) at the end of *chobiyyah* dance patterns.

a.

X		X		X	X		
1	&	2	&	3 e & a	4 e & a		
D	D	D	T	D • • T	• • T •		

b.

X		X		X	X	X	X
1	&	2	&	3 e & a	4 e & a	5 e & a	6 e & a
D	D	D	T	D • • T	• • T •	D • • T	• • T •

Clap (X) the down-beat and recite the drum-tones (*Dum* and *Tek*), and you will feel the cross-rhythmic pull of this motion-generating rhythm. (Refer to "Chapter 36: Cross-Rhythm" in Section V.)

Sometimes *chobiyyah* is called *bambi*. Although similar to *chobiyyah* with a *malfuf*-like rhythm embedded within it, *bambi* is an eight-beat *wahida*-type Egyptian pattern with the pulses divided as 3 + 3 + 3 + 3 + 2 + 2 (which equals 16 pulses). It is typically used as an introductory pattern leading to *baladi*, *maqsum*, or some other similar rhythm. The name is thought to be derived from the Turkish word for the color pink: *pembe*. Why this is so is unknown, although it is possibly due to Iraq's proximity to Turkey. Arabic musicians sometimes use the term *bambi* freely, making identification uncertain. Note that there are variations of *bambi* and *chobiyyah* with extra *Dums* added, which also makes identification difficult. The following notation is an example of a basic version of Egyptian *bambi*:

```
X     X     X     X     X     X     X     X
1  &  2  &  3  &  4  &  5  &  6  &  7  &  8  &
D  .  .  T  .  .  T  .  .  T  .  .  D  .  T  .
```

There are several recordings of *chobiyyah* available, however, the six-beat version is hard to find. Both the six- and four-beat versions are demonstrated on track #9, "Chobie," on Nourhan Sharif's CD *Rhythms from Around the World*, published by the Egyptian Academy of Dance. A recording of the popular Iraqi song called "Shlonak Eyni Shlonak" by the Salatin el Tarab Orchestra, using the four-beat version, is found in several places. It can be heard on the CD *Belly Dance Fever* (HMC12422), track #14; and on *Visit Me in Baghdad* (HMC 1287), track #15 called "Dabke Iraqiyi," available from the Hollywood Music Center.

The same recording is also on Neena and Veena's collection CD called *Essential Belly Dance*, track #13 called "Shlonak," published by Caravan Records. A different piece at a faster tempo called "Doe a tabl," by the Hicham Katir Orchestra, is found on the CD *123 Belly Dance*, vol. 2, track #13. It is published by MLP/World Music Office (Musiques du Monde). A definitive example of *bambi* is demonstrated by Nourhan Sharif on his CD *Rhythms From Around the World*, track #4.

CHAPTER 30: CHOBIYYAH MALFUF—A VARIATION

As discussed in the previous chapter, *Chobiyyah* (cho-BEE-yah) is an Iraqi line dance (of which there are local variations) similar to the Lebanese *debke*, but specific to Iraq instead of Lebanon. Although *chobiyyah* is not belly dance, the principle rhythm of the same name can easily be adapted to modern routines, as have many other patterns such as *debke*.

There is more than one rhythm used for *chobiyyah*. The basic rhythm for *chobiyyah* is *malfuf*—the "rolling" rhythm with the 3 + 3 + 2 structure. *Malfuf* is rendered in one cycle (i.e., one measure) of two beats. The following illustration shows the pattern and form (refer to "Chapter 14: Malfuf" in Section II).

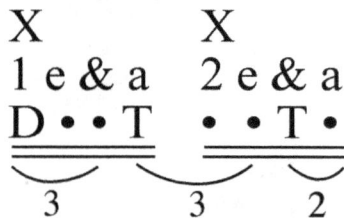

<pre>
    X   X
  1 e & a   2 e & a
  D • • T   • • T •
  ‾‾‾‾‾‾‾   ‾‾‾‾‾‾‾
   3   3   2
</pre>

The common rendition of the *chobiyyah malfuf*, expands the *malfuf* pattern to create a two measure version. This expanded pattern (now four beats long: 2 + 2) is used at the beginning and transitions of sections, and as a simple variation to the monotony of *malfuf* over and over—a useful possibility adaptable to belly dance accompaniment.

The notation at the top of the next page illustrates the pattern and structure of the two measure, four beat *chobiyyah malfuf*.

```
X        X        X        X
1   &    2   &    3 e & a  4 e & a
D   D    D   T    D • • T  • • T •
```
⏝⏝⏝⏝⏝⏝⏝⏝⏝⏝   ⏝⏝⏝⏝⏝⏝⏝⏝⏝⏝
  additional pattern   *malfuf*

A six-beat version (illustrated below) is also danced, though it is less common. The pattern is created by extending the four-beat (two measure) version by two more beats, adding a third measure of *malfuf* rhythm. Thus, the six-beat version has three measures of two beats each: 2 + 2 + 2.

```
X      X      X      X      X      X
1  &   2  &   3 e & a 4 e & a 5 e & a 6 e & a
D  D   D  T   D • • T • • T • D • • T • • T •
```
⏝⏝⏝⏝ ⏝⏝⏝⏝   ⏝⏝⏝⏝ ⏝⏝⏝⏝   ⏝⏝⏝⏝ ⏝⏝⏝⏝
                                  2nd *malfuf*

To learn the *chobiyyah malfuf* rhythm so you can recognize it in recordings or in a live setting, try the following exercise; use the notation as a guide: Clap (X) the down-beats and recite the drum-tones (*Dum* and *Tek*), and you will feel the cross-rhythmic pull of this motion-generating rhythm. (Refer to "Chapter 36: Cross-Rhythm" in Section V.)

CHAPTER 31: DEBKE— THE DANCE AND THE RHYTHM

Group folk dances are a vital part of the repertoire of the belly dance community. Among the many types performed by troupes, such as *khalîji*, an essential dance/rhythm centered in Lebanon is called *debke* (pronounced DEHB-kee, the Lebanese phonetic spelling). Variations of the name come from regional/ local dialects. For example, *dabke* uses an <u>ah</u> instead of an <u>e</u> ("eh") and *dabkeh* alters the ending sound from "kee" to "keh." It is debatable where the *debke* dance form originated. Line dances with the same basic form abound throughout the Middle East and northern Mediterranean. The dance and rhythm described below is the modern Lebanese version.

The *debke* line is formed by each dancer holding hands, putting arms around the waist, on the shoulder, or linking arms with the person on either side. The line is lead by the *raas* (head) who gestures and twirls a handkerchief, scarf, Muslim prayer beads called the *masbha* (similar to the Christian rosary), or a chain in his free right hand. The *raas* leads the line from behind and to the right in meanders and geometries (semi-circles, etc.) throughout the dance space. In addition to the line, the principle characteristic of *debke* is the complex footwork mixing front, back, and side steps, foot crossing, stomping, hopping, kicking, spinning, and dropping to the knees. Indeed, *debke* means, "stomping of the feet" in Arabic. There are reputed to be over a hundred possible step combinations. Each locality has its own flavor of the dance. A friendly competition arises sometimes when the leader tries to outwit the line with more and more complicated steps. At the behest of Lebanese President Camille Chamoun, Igor Moiseyev, a Russian choreographer, designed a "classical" foundation to the

dance steps. (He died in November of 2007 at the age of 101.) The first performance of Moiseyev's formalized *debke* was given by the Al Anwar dance troupe in 1960 at the Baalbeck Festival in Lebanon.

The Lebanese have adopted the *debke* as their national dance. The politicization of the dance has created subtexts of meaning. The lead dancer, with arms outstretched, represents a strong tree (cedar). Hand or shoulder holding, creating a chain, represents the connection and continuity of the people, community, and culture. Foot stomping acknowledges the connection to the land. Outside of the formalized versions performed by professional stage groups in Lebanon, the *debke* is an immanently participatory social dance for all genders and ages at weddings, parties, and gatherings of all types. Participants break in and out of the line, and the leader may change during the course of the dance, which may last several songs.

The origin of the *debke* is unknown, although several theories have been put forth. The Lebanese believe that the *debke* (as they dance it) evolved out of communal winter work-parties during which musicians played to help keep the people going at their tasks. Some have suggested that the Turks adopted it from the Rom, and then spread it during the Ottoman Empire's reign. Another line of thought is that the dance originated among, and was proliferated by, the Kurdish people. During the political split-up of their land, expatriate Kurd refugees settled in the Levant (Lebanon, Syria, Jordan, and Palestine), Iraq, Iran, Turkey, and Armenia.

As noted above, the *debke* can be danced to several rhythms depending upon the locality. The illustration at the top of the next page is one possible version of *sudasi*, set in a six-beat time cycle.

1	&	2	&	3	&	4	&	5	&	6	&
D	D	t k	D	D	t k	D	D	t k	D	T	•

The Sudasi version of the Debke rthythm—implementing a 6-beat cycle

Patterns set in four- or eight-beat time cycles are currently popular. Below, a four-beat time-cycle version of the *debke* rhythm (herein called) is shown. Notice that this rhythm is very similar to the Egyptian *sa'idi* rhythm. Note also that *sudasi* and *debke* are the same essential pattern. The flow rate of the salient beat is from 120 bpm± down to 60 bpm±, depending upon the preference of the dancers, the local style, and energy state of the setting. In modern recordings, electric bass is used to reinforce the low drum-tone (*Dum*) played on the *dumbek* (*tabla*).

1	&	2	&	3	&	4	&
D	D	T	D	D	•	T	•

Four-beat Debke rhythm

A common variant (shown below) leaves out the first drumtone on the down-beat of 1, creating syncopation. The drum's sound is replaced by the dancers' foot stomp on that beat.

1	&	2	&	3	&	4	&
•	D	T	D	D	•	T	•

Four-beat Debke variant, syncopating the first down-beat—replacing it with dancers' foot-stomps

There are many recordings available online. Check out http://www.hollywoodmusiccenter.com and http://www.arabymusic.com for CDs and sound clips. The recording of the performance called "The Black Tents" by the *Caracalla* dance troupe is much-lauded as a documentation of the early 6/4 version of the *dabke* rhythm.

The Lebanese singer Fairouz and the Rahbani brothers' orchestra are associated with the debke's popularity in Lebanon, the Levant, and to wider audiences in the Mediterranean. One of their most well-known songs is "Dabket Loubnan." Another well-known song, performed by many singers, is "Ala Dalouna." Any recordings by Naif Agby and the Lebanese Radio Orchestra (one group) are great, but they are now rare and are collector's albums (keep those old LPs!). Modern *debke* is well represented on the CD "Al-Dabke" by Mohammed Iskandar.

CHAPTER 32: DANSE ORIENTALE BOLÉRO

The influence of Latin and African rhythm on the music of the Middle East is extensive, and the *boléro,* as it is used in *danse orientale,* is no exception. In the *danse orientale* community, dancers know it as the sensuous slow rhythm other than *chiftetelli.* (See Chapter 17: Chiftetelli" in Section II.)) In the ballroom dancing community, a similar form of the *boléro* rhythm is used as a standard repertoire dance where performers are judged for their perfection and passion. There is also a short decorative jacket worn open in the front by ballroom and belly dancers called a *boléro.* In classical music halls, "The Boléro" by Maurice Ravel, with its incessant snare drum part and crescendo lasting from the beginning to the end, is well known. In the 1979 Blake Edwards movie *10* (with Dudley Moore, Bo Derek, and Julie Andrews), Ravel's music is used in the most infamous scene. In rock n' roll, the rhythm can be heard in songs such as Roy Orbison's "Running Scared" and "The Crowd," and Jeff Beck's "Beck's Bolero."

The *danse orientale boléro* rhythm (herein referred to as *DOB* to differentiate it from the other types of *boléro*) has two identifying characteristics, illustrated in the diagram at the top of the next page. The first is that the *DOB* has the rhythmic figure called a *triplet* (an artificial grouping of three notes), placed after the first down-beat (the low-note *Dum*) in the rhythm. The second characteristic is the presence of an accented *Dum* (low note) on the fourth beat. This rhythmic feature appears to tie the *DOB* to the *rumba* rhythm (see below), which has the same emphasis on beat four. These two characteristics are illustrated in the following diagram of the typical *danse orientale* version, sometimes also called the *Arabic boléro,* the *rumboléro,* or the *rumba Arabi* among other mixed names.

1	&	2	&	3	&	4	&
D	tkt	T	k	T	k	D	k

Danse Orientale Boléro, also known as Arabic Boléro or Rhumba Arabi

The original *boléro* is reputed to have been created by Sebastian Cerezo in Cadiz, Spain, around 1780. It is probable he was influenced by the music fusion that resulted from the historical Arabic control of the region (facilitated through Morocco) of southern Spain known as Andalusia. Cerezo's initial form of the *boléro* was set in a time cycle of three beats. It became known as a Spanish solo (male or female) dance in which the dancer also sings and plays the castanets (a Moroccan influence), and had popular currency from the time of its creation and throughout the 1800s. Guitars and tambourines provide the standard instrumental accompaniment. The following example illustrates the Spanish *boléro*.

1	&	2	&	3	&
D	tkt	T	k	D	k

Spanish Boléro

As noted, the *DOB* is connected to the Cuban rhythm called the *rumba*. The traditional Afro-Cuban *rumba* is a multilayered, syncopated rhythm and dance that combines its Congolese drumming roots with Spanish music. There are three types: *guaguanco, Columbia,* and *yambú*, which are played in either a cycle of two or four depending upon the setting. It is interesting to note that the Cuban *rumba* rhythm was taken to southern Spain in the 1800s, and adapted into the forms called *rumba*

gitana or *rumba flamenca*. Brought to Cuba by Spaniards, the *boléro* changed from a three-beat time cycle to a square (perhaps more danceable) time cycle of two beats (or four, depending on how one counts). Two of the rhythm layers present in Cuban *rumba* are the *martillo* (bongo pattern) and the *baqueteo* (timbale pattern). These two patterns have the syncopated displacement emphasis of the bass tone on the fourth beat of the cycle (leading to the One). It is believed that these elements were fused to the Spanish three-beat cycle *boléro*. José Pepe Sánchez wrote the first popular Cuban *boléro* song called "Tristeza" in 1885. The *boléro* was further altered and changed as it traveled through Mexico, and the Central- and South-American regions. In Argentina, it blended with the *tango*, for example. The musical influences of Cuba in New York and Miami, and throughout the world, are vast. The circles of musical migration back and forth between continents and among cultures have created many variants.

Among the European composers (Beethoven, Chopin, Weber, Auber, and Berlioz) who wrote *boléros* (music set to that rhythm) in the style of Cerezo, French composer Maurice Ravel (1875–1937) is the most well-known (see illustration below of Ravel's boléro rhythm). His "The Boléro" (written in a time cycle of four) was created in 1928 for Ida Rubinstein's ballet troupe. Ravel considered it a technical piece, but it's subsequent popularity far exceeded his intentions. In 1937 when he was visiting Morocco, sometime after he wrote the piece, he was surprised to hear the *boléro*-like tune and rhythm being whistled by a man walking along the street. Whether his composition made it to Morocco (which is unlikely since it didn't gain wide popularity until after his death later that same year), or whether the melody and rhythm are inherent to Morocco (more probable) and were the original influence to Cezero via Morocco, is debatable—no research has been successful in finding any such specific melody.

bpm 66 ♩ Tempo di Bolero, moderato assai

Ravel's Boléro rhythm excerpt

The American-style ballroom dance *boléro* rhythm (in four beats) employs the dance steps *slow • quick quick*. "Slow" is supported by the first two figures of the pattern (including the triplet which "floats"). "Quick, quick" is supported by an inverted figure pair in which the second figure is accented rather than the first (the 4TH-beat low pitch). The *ballroom boléro* thus reflects the same structure as the four-beat *danse orientale boléro*, and as suggested, the *rumba*.

As can be seen, the *danse orientale boléro* (DOB) is an international rhythm with many flavors. When listening to the various renditions, notice that the *Dum* on beat four leading to the one, along with the triplet in the first half, create a particular signature that helps to identify the rhythm.

Examples of the *danse orientale boléro* can be heard on John Bilezikjian's *A Thousand and One Nights* CD (Armenian style), and in the Arabic song "Entel Hob" on volume two of the CD *Belly Dance Superstars*. For a Ravelesque/Mexican flavored version, listen to George Abdo's "Sahirnee." Fairuz's version of the song "Ya Mayla Al Ghoussoune" uses a *rumba*-like version. A demonstration of the pattern called *rumba arabi* is on Nourhan Sharif's CD, *Drumming of Lebanon*. There are many available recordings of Ravel's classic "Boléro."

CHAPTER 33: SHISH-HASHT AND BANDARI— PERSIAN RHYTHMS

Iran is a diverse cultural complex whose strongest ethnic component is that of the prevailing Persian culture. Persian classical music is thought to have been synthesized during in the Qajar Period (1785–1925), combining earlier theory and practice, including instrument and technique influences from the Mongol invasions between 1200 to 1400 CE. The folk music of the Baluchi, Kordi, and Gilaki subcultures within Iran, among others, are also important elements. European orchestral and band influences (notation, harmony, counterpoint, and instruments) have been incorporated as well, beginning in the 1800s and continuing into the present within various popular music genres. Although Persian *shish-hasht* (six-eight) is not a typical rhythm used by the belly dance community, and is emphatically *not* used among Iranians for such purposes, increasing numbers of western dancers are using it as a vehicle for performance—in the expanded definition of *danse orientale* as inclusive of more than Arabic and Turkish music and dance. In this article, two forms of six-beat time-cycle rhythm are discussed: *shish-hasht* and *bandari*.

Shish-hasht (pronounced sheesh-HASHT) is the typical rhythm (and eponymous style of music) in Iranian popular music—especially that produced by diaspora immigrants and their descendents in southern California (among other places). It is also the core rhythm for the "reng" (dance) section in classical music suites. The rhythm is sometimes referred to as *shir-e madar* (literally, "milk of the mother")—inferring its importance to Persian cultural identity. Note that the word *shir* also means "lion" in Iranian Farsi. While it is considered most "authentic"

when realized on the *tombak* (see below), it can be played on the *dumbek* (a.k.a. Arabic *tabla*, etc.), western drumset, and electronically.

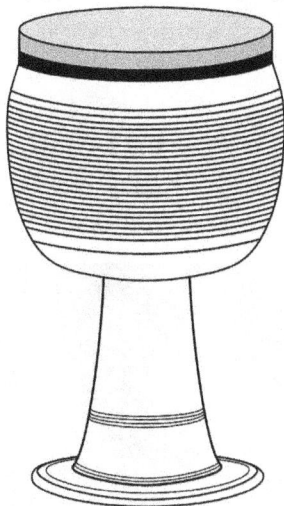

Tombak or Zarb, lathed from wood

The main drum used to play *shish-hasht* is the resonant goblet-shaped *tombak* or *tonbak* (18± inches x 10.5 ± inches). The name derives, like the dumbek, from the two principle tones produced on the drum: *tom* (the low tone) and *bak* (the high tone). The colloquial name for the drum is *zarb*. *Zarb* may be translated variously as "multiplication," "beat," or "rhythm." The name is used to indicate the drum itself, and "to play the beat," i.e., the *zarb*. *Zarb* may also allude to the rolling technique characteristic of *tombak* playing. The tombak has a thicker drumhead than that used for Arabic and Turkish dumbeks (*tabla* and *deblek*), and may be made from cow, camel calf, or sometimes lamb hide. It is manufactured on a lathe from a single aged trunk of hardwood: mulberry, walnut, and more recently *zaban gonjeshk*, a light-colored wood from a tree of the Sycamore family. Its interior

tube and cylinder are sometimes partially chiseled out as well as lathed for the purpose of fine-tuning the instrument. The exterior surface is left unadorned, incised with horizontal bands, or carved with historical bas-reliefs. It is then stained or left natural, and varnished. Some *tombaks* feature complex mosaic designs called *khatam* ("hammered"), laminated onto the surface with sheets of photographically patterned plastic or created by an artist with individual pieces of wood and shell. Mass-produced versions are made from softer woods such as pine. They are constructed of cutout blocks that are glued together, and then lathed.

Helmi-brand tombaks

Persian *tombak* playing style is the most complex among the dumbek family of drums. The acoustics of the large-diameter head of the *tombak*, and the differential between the resonator chamber (the upper part of the drum) to the tube and the waist,

allow for a rich resonance and tonal manipulation not possible on Arabic (*tabla*) and Turkish (*deblek*) dumbeks. The sound of the *tombak* is distinguished by the use of the resonant bass tone called *tom* (similar to *Dum* on the *dumbek*), a treble drum-tone called *kenar bak* played on the straight edge of the drum with fingertips (similar to *tek* on the dumbek) or by a left-handed snapping technique called *pâlang* (leopard). The use of complex finger rolling ornaments (*takriz* and *tazin;* also referred to as *reez*), for example, the *meyaneh bak riz*, the *riz-e pour*, and the *eshareh* leading into *tom*, are important characteristics of *tombak* playing. In classical music, the *tombak* has been taken to the level of the virtuoso by performers such as Ostad Hossein Tehrani (1912–1974), Nasser Farhangfar (1947–1997), Morteza Ayan (1947–), and Jamshid Chemirani (1942–). New master performers include Pejman Hadadi and Peyman Nasehpour, among many others.

The adaptation of Persian *shish-hasht* to the dumbek falls short of the beauty and subtlety possible on the *tombak*. Although Turkish-style dumbeks have a small waist and come closer to emulating the resonant sound of *tom* on a *tombak*, Arabic-type dumbeks do not reproduce the *tom* sound faithfully. The Arabic *tabla* has a wide waist, and therefore less resonance. The finger snap cannot be successfully played on a round edged drum such as the Arabic *tabla* or certain styles of round-edged Turkish *deblek*. Nonetheless, despite the acoustical and physical differences, basic Persian *shish-hasht* patterns can be played on them, and some of the techniques imitated.

A compound-duple meter in a cycle of six, *shish-hasht* is divided into two groups: 3 + 3 with the strong duple pulse marked on the first down-beat of each group of three—**123, 456**. The rhythm is characterized by an emphasis (>) on beats 1, 3, 4, and

5, creating a quality sometimes referred to as *kereshmeh* ("lilt" or "flirt"). In Persian classical music *kereshmeh* also refers to a specific type of rhythmic and melodic structuring. The following example illustrates a basic rendition (adapted from the *tombak* to *dumbek* notation) of the *shish-hasht* pattern without any of the characteristic embellishment. The Xs mark the duple pulse of the compound meter.

X			**X**		
>		**>**	**>**	**>**	
1	**2**	**3**	**4**	**5**	**6**
D	**•**	**T**	**D**	**T**	**•**

The second type of rhythm, *bandari* (Farsi, "from the port," pronounced BAHN-dar-ee), is not "Persian" in the sense that it does not have a provenance connecting it to classical Persian culture. However, it *is* Iranian. *Bandari* is both a musical style and a dance whose original context is found in the ports or harbors (*bandar*) along the Iranian coast in the Persian Gulf. Until around 1965, Iranians knew *bandari* only as a folk music played by oil tanker and refinery workers, stevedores, and other laborers. It is a *syncretic* music—a mixture of Iranian, Arabic, and black African music and movement unique to the Persian Gulf. Other similar forms exist in the Persian Gulf along the coasts of Iraq and the eastern Saudi Peninsula, although it's not called *bandari* or accompanied by singing in Farsi. Variants are also found along the western coast of Africa as far down as Kenya, along the coasts of Pakistan and India, and wherever Iranian sailors traveled.

With the influx of western Rock 'n Roll into Iran in the 1960's (the Beatles and Rolling Stones, etc.), urban musicians in bandar-e Abâdan and bandar-e Abbâs, for example, began to adapt folk music to the electric band. Two of the most well-known songs heard on Iranian radio in 1965 that popularized *bandari* to a wide audience were *Aghasi's* "Ameneh" and *Sandy's* "Dokhtar Ahvazi." This music was brought to the United States by refugees fleeing from the Islamic Revolution, and the Iran/Iraq war (in particular from the bombed-out harbor city of Abâdan). By the mid-1990s, *bandari* had become an established feature in Persian dance clubs in Los Angeles (L.A.) at places such as the *Cabaret Tehran*. In the early days, singers sold homemade cassette recordings at their concerts. *Bandari*, in all its forms can now be enjoyed on YouTube.

Bandari can be loosely separated into two general types: folk and urban. The folk version employs a local bagpipe called the *ney anban, barbat (oud)*, the local decorated wood *tempo arabi* (a type of Arabic *tabla*), *zarb*, anything available for percussion (oil drums, gas cans, or any resonant or sonorous object), Arabic tambourine, and clapping. The *tempo arabi* and *zarb* are sometimes strapped together to make a drum array—hand-held and braced under the arm and against the knee. Urban electric-band *bandari* (L.A. style) is played on electronic keyboards such as those made by the Gem Company. The *ney aban* sound is imitated in the Gem "Oriental" model using the "NayAn" setting, and the onboard rhythm machine is set to "bandary" [1 or 2] with sampled sounds of *zarb* and so on. Other band instruments sometimes include the electric bass and guitar and drumset. Two conga drums (a *quinto* and a *tumba*) and a cast aluminum Arabic style *tabla* (*tempo arabi*) comprise the current favored hybrid percussion stand-mounted arrayfor performing *bandari*.

Typical *bandari* folk lyrics, sung in "call-and-response" style, cover subjects such as loneliness—an oil tanker captain or oil platform boss and his men singing about wanting to go home to their wives or girlfriends. Modern urban song texts range from love and work to implied political and social commentaries. The lead singer of the band will often put the names of the host of the party and their friends into the lyrics. In live performance, *bandari* songs are frequently chained together forming a set of twenty minutes or longer.

The modern urban dance form of *bandari* is characterized by various combinations of raised arms (above the shoulders), forward and back motion of the upper torso while rotating or shaking the head and shoulders, moving the feet in either a forward/back, side-to-side, or mixed shuffle, danced individually, in couples, or in a traveling circle. In the circle form, individuals step into the center and dance before exchanging places with another. There is joyful shouting and interlocking hand clapping by both dancers and audience participators. In the *danse orientale* community, *bandari* has become an addition to other folk dances such as *khalîji* (see "Chapter 27: Khalîji" in this Section). Iranians may also refer to *bandari* as *khalîji*.

Like *shish hasht*, the core pattern of *bandari* is set in a time cycle of six beats, played as compound-duple meter divided into two groups: 3 + 3. The duple pulse is accented on the first down-beat of each group of three—123, 456. *Bandari* is not played with florid embellishments like *shish-hasht*. It also does not have the accents on 1, 3, 4, 5 like *shish-hasht*. Bandari's complete form is phrased in a recurring binary (6 + 6) "question/answer" rotation. The first cycle begins with a low tone, and the second cycle begins with a high tone. *Bandari* has a shifting rhythmic feel derived from the African *hemiola* (two beats "against" three beats). Folk-style

tempi tend to be slower around 85 bpm±; urbanized *bandari* is faster at around 126 bpm±. There are several interpretations (styles) of *bandari*, depending upon the musicians' locality of origin.

Although playable on a single drum, at least two drums (*zarb* and *tempo arabi*) are preferred (as noted above), perhaps reflecting the influence of sub-Saharan Africa. The following example illustrates a rendition of the Abadani influenced L.A.-style as played on a three-drum array using a *tempo arabi* (Arabic *tabla*), and two conga drums (*quinto* and *tumba*). Note that *bandari* is not embellished like *shish-hasht* with complex rolls (*takriz*), snaps (*pâlang*), and tonal variations. *Bandari*, when played by two or more drummers, benefits from polyphonic variation. The Xs represent the duple pulse of the compound meter.

Key

D = Dum, T = Tek

q = quinto open tone

t = tumba open tone

x			x			x			x		
1	2	3	4	5	6/	1	2	3	4	5	6/
D	T	q	T	t	t	T	T	q	T	t	t

L.A.-style Bandari drum array (Shahin Tavili, musician/singer)

The *shish-hasht* and *bandari* patterns presented here are the basic forms. As already suggested above, the performance of these musical types (and rhythms) depend upon the context. Dock workers hanging out with friends after work will play *bandari* differently than the dance–music-style blasted through speakers in a nightclub. There are regional differences as well. The same is true for the many variants of *shish-hasht*, which can be found

in folk, classical, and popular music. While variations of the *bandari* rhythm comes from natural polyphony (several people playing the rhythm), the complex embellishment of the *shish-hasht* rhythm on the *tombak* is learned through study. In classical music, for example, the placement of *riz-e pour* (full *reez*) and *eshareh* (roll leading into a main drum-tone such as *tom*) has an important relationship to melody and words. When listening to either of these rhythms, listen for the duple beats (1 and 4) that define the primary cyclic structure—**1** 2 3, **4** 5 6. To gain a better understanding of the varieties, go to YouTube and type in keywords "bandari," shish-hasht," and "Persian six-eight," and they will lead you to numerous examples.

Bandari Players: R–L—Jamshid Nowzari, Ali Sadr, Dara Bamoradi

Belly Dance Rhythm Resource

SECTION V
DANCE MUSIC ANALYSIS

Belly Dance Music Is Influenced by Music and Dance World-Wide

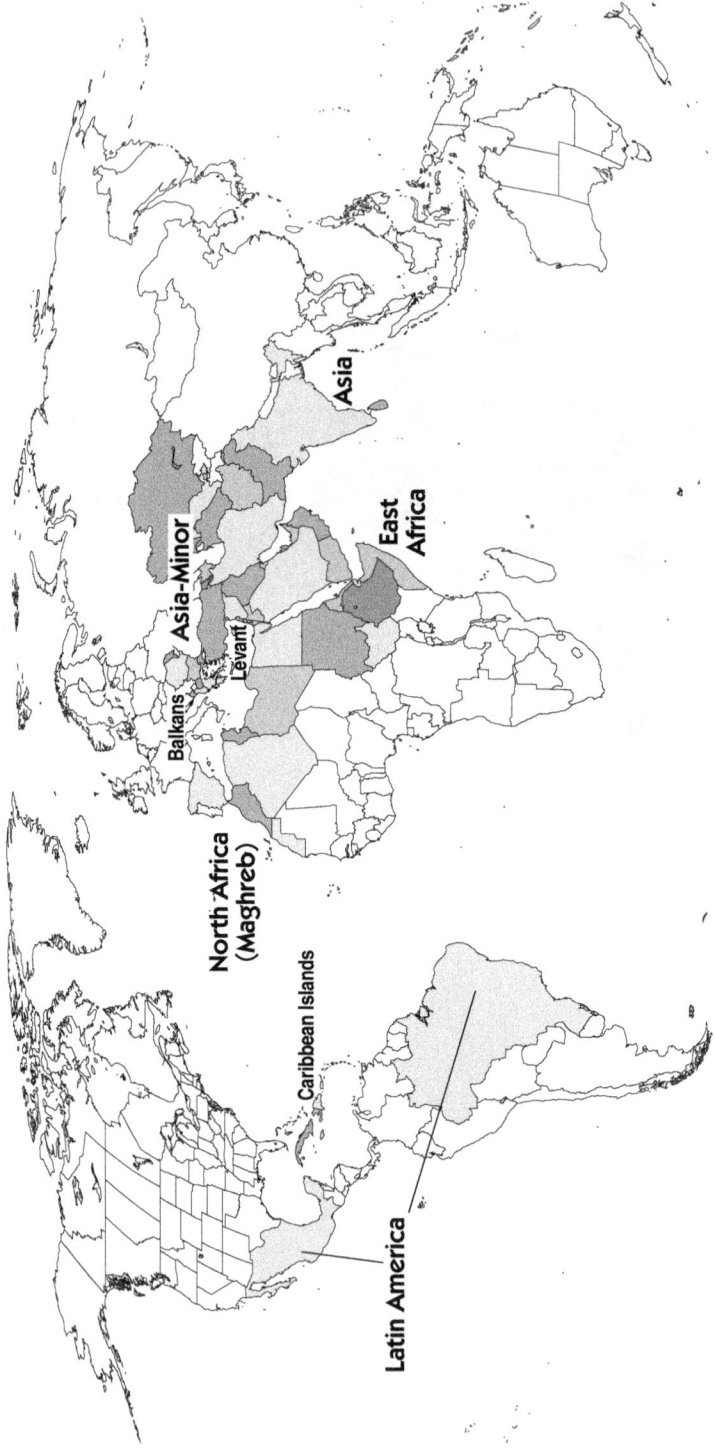

Asia

Asia-Minor

East
Africa

Balkans

Levant

North Africa
(Maghreb)

Caribbean Islands

Latin America

CHAPTER 34: RELATIONSHIPS—MASMUDI

Relationships can be confusing. Is that *sa'idi* or is that *baladi*? *Fellâhi* sounds like *maqsum*, but played really fast! How can you tell which is which, since they seem to be so similar? Why is one faster and the other slower, and why is the same rhythm played at different speeds?

First, they *are* similar in that they derive from a rhythm called *masmudi*. The eight-beat cycle pattern called *masmudi kabir* (large) is believed to have derived from a rhythm among the *Masmuda*, an ancient tribal confederacy of agricultural Berbers living in the western part of North Africa. Western Arab court musicians in 13TH century Morocco and Tunisia first adapted the rhythm to the Classical vocal suite called the *muwashahat* (Arabic for "girdled"). An alternate name for the rhythm is *masmudi taweel*, referring to the three *dums* in its sequence. *Masmudi saghir* (small) a.k.a. *baladi* is spread over a cycle of four beats instead of eight. *Masmudi kabir's* other derivative rhythms, *maqsum, fellâhi,* and *sa'idi,* have already been discussed in detail in previous chapters.

Although the diagram and table offered below showing the relationships and differences between the members of the *masmudi* family of rhythms may be a bit technical for some, please make an effort to study it; it will greatly enhance your understanding of belly dance rhythms. A simple visual perusal will reveal the relationships and differences. You don't have to be a literate musician to understand. Once you see these relationships and differences in the diagram and table, try some active listening. Can you identify the rhythm? Find the down-beat and clap along with it, then count. What is the time cycle?

How many down-beats are there in the time cycle of the rhythm in the music?

The time cycles of the *masmudi* family compared in Diagram 1, below, range from an eight-beat cycle (*masmudi*) to a four-beat cycle (*baladi, maqsum,* and *sa'idi*), to a two-beat cycle (*fellâhi*). There is nothing complicated here, since these common "square" time cycles are embedded in our Western culture. Most of the popular music heard on the radio and elsewhere is set in cycles derived from two (two, four, eight, twelve, sixteen) and three (three and six). As a belly dancer, you are exposed to many other time cycles. Take some time to learn how to figure out a cycle; it's not hard to do, but it does takes concentration and practice! *Listen* to dance rhythms. Can you recognize the basic "melody" of drum-tones made up of the bass-pitch *Dum* (the near-center of the drum), and the treble drum-tone, *Tek* (the edge of the drum)? Can you recite the basic rhythm while you clap your hands to the time cycle?

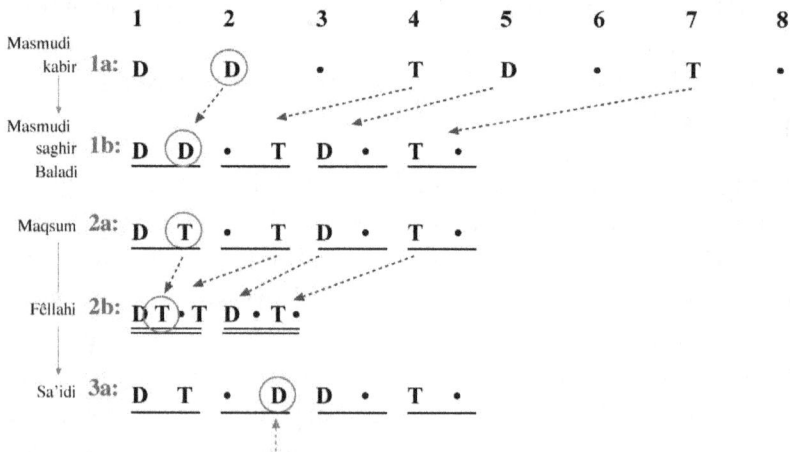

		1	2	3	4	5	6	7	8
Masmudi kabir	1a:	D	(D)	•	T	D	•	T	•
Masmudi saghir / Baladi	1b:	D	(D)	•	T	D	•	T	•
Maqsum	2a:	D	(T)	•	T	D	•	T	•
Fêllahi	2b:	D	T	• T	D	•	T	•	
Sa'idi	3a:	D	T	•	(D)	D	•	T	•

Diagram 1 *Relationships of the rhythmic patterns generated from the five drum-tone rhythm (DD-TD-T-) masmudi kabir*

Diagram 1 illustrates the relationships of the rhythmic patterns generated from the five drum-tone rhythm (DD-TD-T-) *masmudi kabir*. The *masmudi* family of rhythms is categorized into three groups: **1** (**a**, **b**), **2** (**a**, **b**), and **3** (**a**). *Masmudi kabir* (**1a**) generates *masmudi saghir* also known as *baladi* (**1b**). The reduction of *masmudi's* eight-beat cycle to *baladi's* four-beat cycle, is reflected in the formal names of the two rhythms: *kabir* (large) and *saghir* (small). In *maqsum* (**2a**), the second drum-tone *Dum* of *masmudi* is replaced by a *tek* (circled). *Maqsum* generates *fellâhi* (**2b**). *Fellâhi* is the same pattern as *maqsum*. The reduction of *maqsum's* four-beat cycle to *fellâhi's* two-beat cycle is the same as the *kabir* and *saghir* reduction in *masmudi*. Finally, the four-beat rhythm *sa'idi* (**3a**) is generated from *maqsum*, and made by substituting the third *Tek* drum-tone in the sequence of *maqsum* with a *Dum* (circled).

Track title	Artist	Album title	Description	Tempo
Masmudi kabir (8 bt cycle) = 110± to 130±				
Masmudi	Issam	The Dancing Drum	masmudi	130±
Masmoudi	Issam	The Dancing Drum	3 dum masmudi	112±
Masmudi saghir aka baladi (4 bt cycle) = 100± to 120±				
Baladi	Issam	The Dancing Drum	baladi	105±
Ali Ashamayel	Fairuz	Fairuz	baladi	98±
Baladi seghir	Abdel Hazim & Abed Halabi	Hatshepsut and other dances	baladi	105±
Noora Noora	George Abdo	Best of George Abdo	baladi	125±
Maqsum (4 bt cycle) = 110± to 150±				
Raks Mustapha	George Abdo	The Best of George Abdo	baladi or maqsum	125±
Maqsoum	Abdel Hazim & Abed Halabi	Hatshepsut and other dances	maqsum	150±
Ghaneyt Ashanak	Gizira Band	Ya Halawa	maqsum	138±
Maqsoum maksoom	Issam	The Dancing Drum	maqsum	130±
Beirut Rythms	Jalilah	In A Beirut Mood (Raks Sharki 6)	maqsum	128±
Layla	Voyager Series	Beyond The Desert	maqsum	110±
Ahlam Beck	Arabic	Ya Salam Ya Fahtiem	maqsum	126±
Fêllahi (2 bt cycle) = 100± to 120±				
Falahi	Mahmoud Fadl	Drummers of the Nile	fêllahi	120±
Falahi	Issam	The Dancing Drum	fêllahi	112±
Fallahi	Issam	The Dancing Drum	fêllahi	128±
Sa'idi (4 bt cycle) = 98± to 130±				
Bethuhshny	Amir Diab	Amarain	pop saidi	130±
Welsa Bethibah/	Amir Diab	Amarain	pop saidi	96±
Saaidi	Hazim & Halabi	Hatshepsut and other dances	pop saidi	130±
Saidi Ya Bouy	Egyptian Artists Sharif & Ali	Wash Ya Wash (Volume 5)	trad. saidi	110±
Ansak Da Kalam	Hossam Ramzy	Egypt	trad. saidi	110±

Table 1 *Comparison of Rhythm Tempos*

Why are these rhythms related to each other, and why are they different? The simple answer is that it is traditional common practice. Tempi vary as can be seen in **Table 1** on the previous page, but the rhythmic pattern remains.

Musicians choose the rate of tempo of any given dance rhythm based upon tradition, situation, and intent. These choices have consequences. Dancers know that the rate of the down-beats has a direct effect upon motion and emotion. The tempi ranges shown in **Table 1** are approximate. They have been averaged from measuring numerous recordings, the author's personal experience, and corroboration with dancers. **Table 1** is partial list—grouped by rhythm—of musical examples that demonstrate the tempo differences between the rhythms. The tempo rate is herein measured at quarter-note down-beats per minute (*bpm*—also known as *mm* or Maezel's Metronome). Using the comparison diagram of the *masmudi* family above as a reference for the patterns, try listening, then clap and count to the examples in **Table 1**. If you can't find the suggested examples illustrating the groups listed here, seek others. Listen to the library of music you have collected in order to find examples of each of these rhythms. There are many sound clips online. Listen to live performances and apply your rhythmic skills. What are the cycles and rhythms?

CHAPTER 35: RHYTHMIC AMBIVALENCE

Ambivalence in rhythm is a device used to invoke dynamic shifting patterns. Typical examples of this effect can be heard in "Latin" music. The *clavé* pattern is a classic example of rhythmic ambivalence being used to create rhythmic dynamism (see "Chapter 14: Malfuf" in Section II)). The shifting feel of the beat as both three and two in the *clavé* rhythm provides a rich source of implied patterns dancers may draw upon to express their motions. Combination of groups of two and three pulses found in the *clavé*, are also used to create ambivalence in other rhythms. In this article, the cyclic grouping of the basic building block of three into cycles of six and twelve will be shown to provide a perfect source for creating rhythmic ambivalence.

The foundation for the musical time-system used for belly dance is simple. It is based upon the most common primary building blocks of time patterning: 2 (binary) and 3 (ternary).

The fundamental unit of musical time is the *pulse*. Undifferentiated pulse has no structure or form: *tick, tick, tick, tick,* and so on.

Once an unaccented pulse is perceived by the listener to have at least one variation, a binary (two-based) form is created. A familiar sonic example of this time-form is the ticking of an analog pendulum-type clock: *tick, tock*. A physical analogy is the alternation of walking: right left.

binary

ternary

A ternary (three-based) form is created by adding a third pulse. An analogy for three is the triangle. Three implies a third dimension of action or space. Binary forms suggest a linear dimension side-to-side, up and down, backwards and forewords, left and right motion. The ternary form thus adds a third dimension. An example of this in dance is the combined motions of traveling through the room or rotating while shimmying side-to-side.

Chaining repetitions of time cycles forms the fundamental organizing format of musical time. The kind of time cycle (that is, the number of beats that make up its parts) determines the basic quality of the time field. The next two examples (a, b) show a chain of twos (a), and a chain of threes (b). Basic un-patterned cycles are denoted by an accent on the first beat: **1**, 2, **1**, 2, **1**, 2, **1**, 2 and **1**, 2, 3, **1**, 2, 3, **1**, 2, 3, **1**, 2, 3.

As noted in the introduction, groupings based upon the basic block of three provide a perfect source for creating rhythmic ambivalence. This phenomenon is most noticeable when combining three in single pairs (3 + 3 = 6) and double pairs (3 + 3 [6] + 3 + 3 [6] = 12). Twelve is—for all intents and purposes—6 + 6, a binary phrase. "Question/Answer" or Call/Response" binary phrasing is a typical method of realizing rhythmic patterns. The

sonic realization of this is to use the low pitch on the down-beat of the pattern for the first iteration, and the high pitch (or some other different sound as a contrast) on the down-beat of the pattern for the second iteration.

The following three examples (a, b, c) show groupings of three unified in cyclic form.

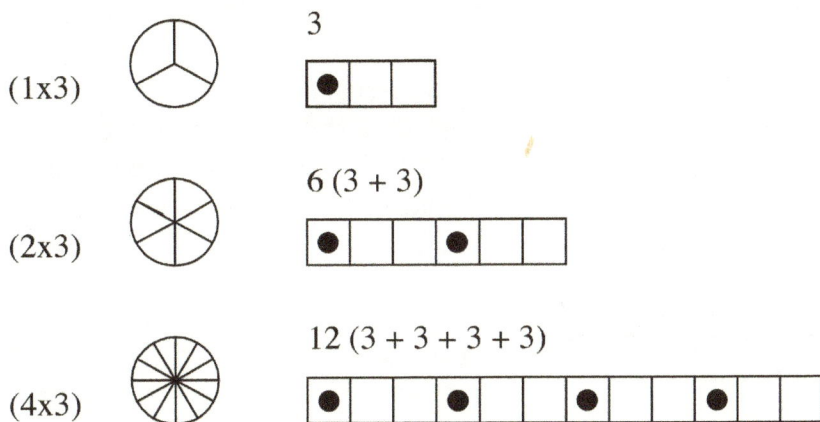

(1x3)   3

(2x3)   6 (3 + 3)

(4x3)   12 (3 + 3 + 3 + 3)

In the next set of illustrations (a, b, c), a cycle of six (a) and a cycle of twelve (b) illustrate binary grouping by twos. The third example (c) shows grouping by fours (2 x 2 = 4).

Note that in all three examples, the down-beat accent (the "one") of the groups forms into sets of threes. The contrast of grouping twos across threes is a basic component of cross-rhythmic interplay (see "Chapter 36: Cross-Rhythm" in this Section).

grouping by 2s

$2 + 2 + 2 = 6$

$2 + 2 + 2 + 2 + 2 + 2 = 12$

grouping by 4s

$4 + 4 + 4 = 12$

In the final example, binary and ternary are alternated, creating a cycle concatenation (series) that shifts between two threes (3 +3) and three twos (2 + 2 + 2). This sequence is a binary phrase composed of one cycle of 6 made of two parts: 3 + 3, and one cycle of 6 made of three parts: 2 + 2 + 2.

grouping by 3s and 2s

$3 + 3 + 2 + 2 + 2 = 12$

There are many interesting interpretations of where to place a movement and an accent while dancing to time-forms using three as the basis for the underlying structure. Patterns in a cycle of six and its double, twelve, can be interpreted as having regular accents (based on groups of two or four) or irregular accents (based upon groups of three) or both at the same time. It is this ambivalence that makes three-based forms a rhythmically dynamic environment for dance expression.

CHAPTER 36: CROSS-RHYTHM

Cross-rhythms are a fundamental aspect of belly dance music. Cross-rhythm occurs when two different rhythms are played at the same time. The term is typically applied when the two rhythms seem to "pull" against the other. Another term for this effect is called *syncopation* (displacement of an expected beat).

The rhythmic pattern called *malfuf* provides a useful example to illustrate cross-rhythm. *Malfuf*, set in a cycle of four beats, consists of three groups of uneven segments (pulses) arranged as 3 + 3 + 2; illustrated herein in time unit box (TUB) notation. The structural arrangement of three uneven groups of pulses is by nature cross-rhythmic when placed in a cycle of eight pulses set into four binary groups, felt as four down-beats (a.k.a. the *tactus*) at a medium tempo (8:4).

The diagram at the right illustrates a cycle of eight pulses grouped as 2 + 2 + 2 + 2.

The diagram below shows the same thing in TUB-style notation. The even continuity of the four beats of the cycle sets up an expectation of regularity—indicated by the arrows.

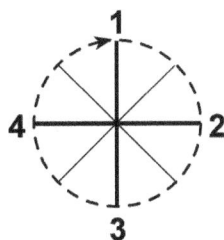

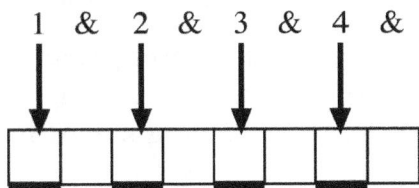

TUB-style notation illustrating a four-beat cycle

The relationship between the regular *tactus* (the down-beat) of the cycle of four, and the irregular accents that denote the first beat of each group of the segments 1, 2, 3, 1, 2, 3, 1, 2) that form *malfuf*, is at the heart of the cross-rhythmic interplay. The following diagram illustrates these connections.

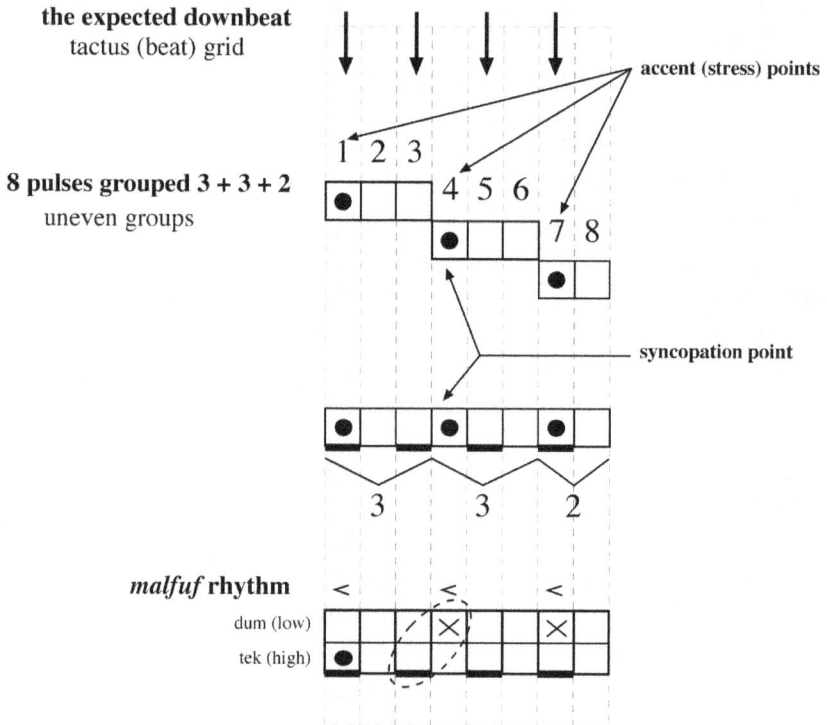

Syncopation—irregular accents—are the foundation of cross-rhythm

As can be seen above, the *malfuf* pattern with its uneven grouping has an accent occurring on the up-beat of the second beat (circled in the diagram). This displacement (*syncopation*) produces the feeling of cross-rhythm.

Cross-rhythmic interplay in belly dance music is a significant element in creating the sense of activity and motion in the music. As an exercise, clap a regular four-beat cycle. Subdivide each beat into a down-beat and up-beat: 1 & 2 & 3 & 4 & (this equals eight pulses). Then, recite the *malfuf* rhythm (*Dum, Tek, Tek*) as shown in the notation above while maintaining the cycle by clapping. You will feel the "pull" of the *malfuf* pattern against the regularity of the cycle.

CHAPTER 37: THE HIDDEN RHYTHM

Like the "hidden" Mickeys of Disneyland, there's a pattern embedded in many belly dance rhythms that most don't know is even there. Is this pattern disguised on purpose like those Mickeys in Disneyland? No, but it does present an interesting musical question. What is this hidden pattern?

Hidden rhythm is an accented arrangement of durations that scan, like poetic prosody, into a sequence of long, long, short. In music, this is manifested as pulses or beats grouped into a sequence of $3 + 3 + 2 = 8$. It is interesting to note that $3 + 3 + 2$ is the Euclidean rhythm E (3, 8). This 3 3 2 sequence is explicit in three belly dance rhythms, and embedded in others. It also is prevalent in Hispanic music.

First, to understand how this sequence of durations is set to a time cycle, try the following exercise. Clap your hands, establishing steady down-beats in a cycle of four. Count "one, two, three, four" as you clap. Then, subdivide each beat in half (up-beats). Count as "one, and, two, and, three, and, four, and." By subdividing each regular down-beat into two, you have created eight pulses.

clap:	X		X		X		X	
count:	1		2		3		4	
count:	1	&	2	&	3	&	4	&

Next substitute the word scheme "one, and..." etc., with the following sequence: "one, two, three, one, two, three, one, two."

This is the 3 3 2 pattern. The 3 3 2 grouping is marked by a dynamical note-stress (an accent) on the down-beat of each set of grouped pulses: "ONE, two, three, ONE, two, three, ONE, two." The three hit accents characterize the pattern.

As you clap and recite (stressing the "ones"), notice how the second "one" of the pattern occurs on the "and" of beat two in the time cycle, and the third "one" of the pattern lands on the fourth beat of the cycle. This is a classic example of syncopation— the asymmetrical accents of the pattern struggle against the regular down-beats of the cycle. Practice this pattern until it becomes natural. *Hint:* try walking and reciting this pattern. In its application to dancing, you must feel the subdivision of the down-beats.

clap:	X		X		X		X	
4 cycle:	1	&	2	&	3	&	4	&
accent:	>			>			>	
332 pattern:	1	2	3	1	2	3	1	2

Recognize anything about this pattern yet? In belly dance music, the 3 3 2 rhythm manifests as *pop-khalîji*, *ayyub*, and *malfuf*. The following diagram illustrates the 3 3 2 pattern in relationship to these rhythms. Note that *pop-khalîji* is set in a time cycle of four beats, whereas *ayyub* and *malfuf* are set in a time cycle of two beats. It is the same pattern scheme but with four subdivisions per beat. Clap on the denoted down-beats of each cycle shown below, and recite the pattern. Drum-tone words: D = Dum, T = Tek, t = tak, k = ka. Note that the wording of *malfuf* is based upon playing the rhythm with alternating hands (r = right, l = left).

When speaking the drum-tone words in *malfuf, ta* and *ka* can be spoken as "t" or "k" or simply as a "tch" sound, instead of saying the words; this makes it easier to say. The important words are *Dum* and *Tek*. (• = a space with no sound)

hits:	↓			↓			↓	
332 pattern:	1	2	3	1	2	3	1	2
pop-khalîjî (4)	D 1	•	•	D 2	•	•	T 3	• 4
ayyub (2)	D 1	•	•	T	D 2	•	T	•
malfuf (2)	D (r 1	k l	t r	T l	t r 2	k l	T r	k l)

For those interested, the 3 3 2 pattern also provides an interesting subject for analysis of the connectivity between so-called Middle-Eastern rhythms and those of Hispanic music. The general consensus is that the Arabs (no doubt influenced by sub-Saharan music) brought the 3 3 2 into the Iberian Peninsula (circa 800 CE). The resulting Spanish-Andalusian culture absorbed it and incorporated it into their music. Spaniards and Portuguese explorers then brought it to the Americas in their music. In Latin music, this hidden pattern is called the *tresillo*. It is a kind of quasi-triplet. That is, it's not really three against two, but it is similar. The *tresillo* is embedded as the 3-side of the 3-2 *son clavé*.

The *clavé* (CLAH-vey, meaning "key" or "keystone," in Spanish) is named after the instrument used to play it. The *clavés* are a pair of sonorous wood cylinders (1" x 6"). The *clavé* pattern, as it is typically called, is the underpinning of *Salsa,* among other Latin music forms. In Mexican music, the 3 3 2 pattern can be heard as an accented guitar chord rhythm in songs such as *Guantanamera* (Girl from Guantánamo). A variant of *tresillo,* a five-hit pattern called *cinquillo* (with five accents counted: 1 • 3, 1 • 3, 1 •), is inherent in the North American boogie-woogie bass line. Both the three- and five-hit variant are found in *rock 'a billy,* and other early *rock 'n roll* forms, as a bass-line as well as a drumset groove. The 3 3 2 grouping is also found in some Asian music. It may be one of the most widespread rhythmic patterns among humans on Earth.

The next time you dance, or just listen to music, can you find the "hidden" 3 + 3 + 2 (long, long, short) pattern?

CHAPTER 38: BELLY DANCE RHYTHMIC PATTERNS—VISUALIZATION

Visualizing sound is an old way of understanding how it relates to time and space. Each one of the following patterns and notation types described herein, has been discussed in previous chapters of this book. Here, the intent is show how each of these patterns look using three types of notation all collected together in one illustration—to reveal different aspects of form and structure.

Each rhythm notation collective is illustrated in the following order:

Time Unit Boxes (TUBs)

- groups—showing the segments
- flat—showing rhythm but no pitch
- pitched—showing drum-tone pitches
  (• = low [*dum*], X = high [*tek*])

Cipher Notation

- letters represent drum-tone notes

Western Notation

- uses note value symbols

We'll use the first two examples, *ayyub* and *malfuf*, to illustrate how the grouping of the segments can reveal a fundamental difference. *Ayyub* is grouped 4 + 2 + 2, whereas, *malfuf* is grouped 3 + 3 + 2. Both are shown here set in a two-beat cycle. Further analysis reveals that the only difference in drum-tones between

them is the *Dum* on beat two. In *malfuf*, the omission of the *Dum* allows the patterns to emphasize the 3+3+2 and have a "rolling" feel, whereas, in *ayyub*, the 4+2+2 structure imparts a "stable" quality to the rhythm. Since these two patterns are so close, it is easy for a musician to shift back and forth between them.

Malfuf

grouped TUBs

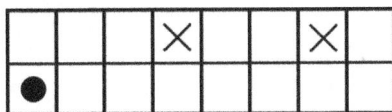

flat TUBs

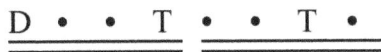

pitched TUBs

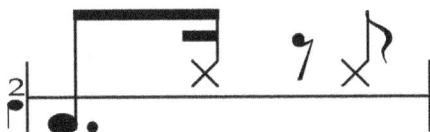

cipher

Western

Malfuf rhythm illustrating 3+3+2 pattern

Ayyub

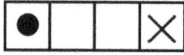

grouped TUBs

flat TUBs

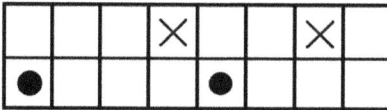

pitched TUBs

cipher

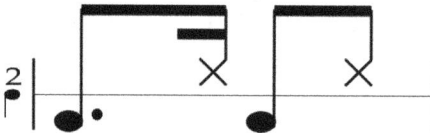

Western

Ayyub rhythm, depicting 4+2+2 pattern

The illustration below, *khalîji [sic in diagram]* shows another 3 + 3 + 2 grouping set in a four-beat cycle. In this case, the grouping is fundamental to the rhythm, and has no ambiguity.

Khalîgi

grouped TUBs

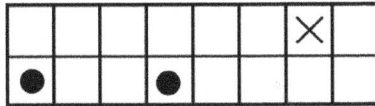

flat TUBs

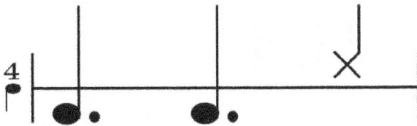

pitched TUBs

D • • D • • T •   cipher

Western

Khalîji rhythm, depicting 3+2+2 pattern

Grouping, as has been implied above, influences the way a rhythm is realized by the musician. *Chiftetelli* (set in an eight-beat cycle), can be interpreted as made-up of four sets of four (4 + 4 + 4 + 4) or as one set of 3+3+2 plus one set of 2 + 2 + 4. In general, Turkish, Greek, Armenian interpretations favor the contrast between the 3+3+2 / 2+2+4 form, whereas the Arabic-Egyptian interpretation tends to emphasize the quadratic nature of the 4+4+4+4 form.

Chiftetelli

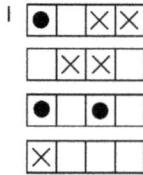

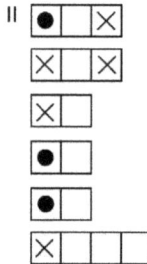

grouped TUBs

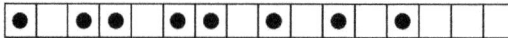

flat TUBs

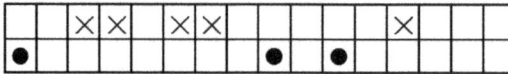

pitched TUBs

D • T T • T T • D • D • T • • •

cipher

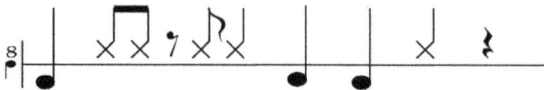

Western

Chiftetelli rhythm

The last two examples, the nine-beat *karshlamá* and the ten-beat *jurjuna*, illustrate "additive" groupings forming odd-numbered cycles. Odd-numbered cycles, when paired, form stable (symmetrical) forms. A valuable aspect to note in these examples is how the low and high drum-tones demarcate the structure. These pillar points (accented by the musician) are auditory cues for dancers, and is present in all rhythms used for belly dance.

Karshlama

grouped TUBs

flat TUBs

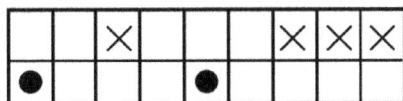

pitched TUBs

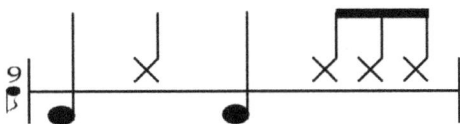

cipher

Western

Karshlama rhythm in 9/8

Jurjuna

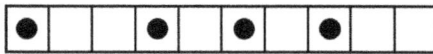

grouped TUBs

flat TUBs

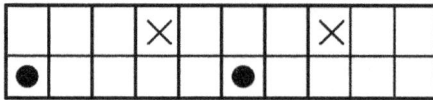

pitched TUBs

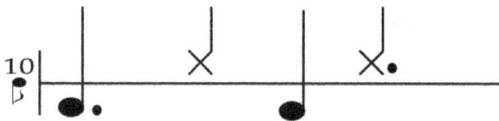

D • • T • D • T • •   cipher

Western

Jurjuna rhythm in 10/8

Although reading notation may seem unnecessary for a dancer to know, do not discount its value as a purely visual way of "seeing" the sound patterns that provide the foundation for your dance. You will be a better dancer for your efforts.

CHAPTER 39: *RAKS MUSTAPHA—*
ANALYSIS OF A CLASSIC BELLY DANCE ROUTINE

The musical suite called "Raks Mustapha," (also sometimes spelled *Mustafa*) as performed by *George Abdo and his Flames of Araby Orchestra*, can be used as a model to demonstrate the sequence of rhythms found in a classic belly dance routine. A suite, as applied to belly dance and the musical accompaniment, means a sequence of dances (a routine) set to rhythmically driven musical pieces (or the other way around: music set to dances). Abdo was among the first to make records with routines for belly dancers available in the West, and although this recording (~1975) is somewhat trite sounding to 21ST-century ears, dance instructors still use it as a basic routine (the sequence, rhythm recognition, the passions) to teach beginning students. "Raks Mustapha" is used at dance recitals as a stand-by classic.

Belly dance musical suites are often set around one or two songs, with rhythmic and melodic instrumental interludes and transitions placed between them. "Raks Mustapha" is set around the song called "Mustapha" or "Ya Mustapha," or "Mustapha Ya Mustapha." The melody is believed to be indigenous to Morocco, and therefore, quite old. The first modernized recording of the song (lyrics added to the melody) was by *Bob Azzam and His Orchestra* (Barclay and Azzam, 1960, France). The style is constructed from so-called Oriental elements (imitation of scale, melody, rhythm, instruments) superimposed over the internationally popular foxtrot dance. As the song and style gained favor, it passed around through the international community. The original song texts were altered during this process, in part due to musicians learning the words by ear (phonetically). The results of such alterations to the lyrics of "Mustapha" range from

serious, dada-istic, funny, silly, raunchy, and gibberish-like. The interesting mixture of languages (Arabic-French-Italian-English) in the lyrics used by Abdo, and by John Bilezikjian (who covers "Mustapha" on his CD *Tapestry of the Dance*, 1997), reflects the song's international currency.

The text of the chorus is an example of the international character and lyric distortion of the song. The following compares the original Azzam words from the chorus (**A**) to the altered words shared by Abdo and Bilezikjian (**B**).

A. [Azzam lyric]
Chéri je t'aime chéri je t'adore,
como la salsa de pomodoro. {2x}

Ya Mustapha, ya Mustapha
Anavaé badia Mustapha
Ça va chérim faila attaarim
Éronquérim matché éma hatchim.

B. [Abdo, Bilezikjian lyric]
Chérie, je t'aime, Chérie, je t'adore,
como la salsa del pommodore. {2x}

Ya Mustapha, ya Mustapha
Ya baheback, ya Mustapha.
Sabaa senine fel Attarine,
Delwati guina Chez Maxim's.

The form of "Raks Mustapha" is derived from its main sections as outlined below. Using letters to stand for each section, the form is ABCDA. Essentially it is a ternary form—ABA—in which B

functions as a derivative extension and expansion of A's rhythmic and melodic materials. In the specific outline below, the musical term *bar* means a single iteration of a 4-beat cycle.

8-bar instrumental pickup into song:

A: "Mustapha" in the *maqsum* rhythm (4-beat cycle), has 2-bar instrumental transitions between lyric sets, slows down at end

B: Oud *taxim* (rhythmically-free improvisation)

C: Slow instrumental melody in *chiftetelli* rhythm (8-beat cycle), speeds up at end leading into drum solo

D: Drum solo begins in *chiftetelli* (8-beat cycle), then shifts to *baladi* (4-beat cycle) with support drums added, and finally to a two-beat cycle over which the drummer plays rhythmic "shimmy" accents and riffs. Ends with a full stop.

5-bar instrumental pickup into song:

A: "Mustapha" reprise in *maqsum* rhythm (4-beat cycle), has 2-bar instrumental transitions between lyrics sets, slows down at the end.

While listening to this recording (Abdo) and following the form as outlined above, count the time cycle on the fingers. Learn the rhythms, *maqsum* and *chiftetelli,* by reciting them. Keep the beat steady (synchronize) along with the tempo and rhythm as they change between sections. The symmetrical (question/answer) arrangement of the measures of the music and lyrics will become apparent—symmetry is common to most belly dance rhythms. Is there a structure to the drum solo? Yes, it starts slowly using the last section's rhythm, then speeds up to the *baladi* segment, then gets fast in the last part (the shimmy), then makes a clear stop.

The drum solo is shaped so that it starts with a big eight-beat cycle, then shifts to four, and finally to a small two-beat cycle while increasing in speed to the end.

Using these concepts and methods with any music (listening actively to the structure and form) will help the dancer recognize rhythms, and to be able to shift between cycles and tempi easier by tuning their ears and body to the sense of the rhythms—this applies to the beginner up to the advanced dancer. By knowing such musical inner structure and outer form, dancers can channel their physical/spatial expression of the music.

This article is based upon the eleven-minute piece titled "Raks Mustapha" on *The Joy of Belly Dancing,* by George Abdo and his Flames of Araby Orchestra (LP; 1975, Monitor Records, New York, NY; Stereo MFS 764; "Music of the Middle-East" series; track #4 on side B). Copies of Abdo's "Raks Mustapha" recording are available online as MP3s, and on hard media—CD, LP, and audio cassette.

CHAPTER 40: LIVE DRUM SOLOS

The drum solo is a highlight of the *orientale* dance routine. Moving against and with the rhythmic "arabesque in the moment," the dancer is at her highest degree of skill. In western *danse orientale* (as it exists in clubs and other venues), there are at least three basic scenarios in which the drum solo occurs. The first is when a dancer chooses a recorded dance music routine that has a drum solo in it, played over the sound system at the restaurant, club, wedding, showcase, etc. By using prerecorded music, the dancer has the opportunity to practice the solo and choreograph it to prepare for a show. Some dancers detail every move and perform it the same way (more or less) each time; other dancers allow for a freer interpretation each time. For either case, the dancer has foreknowledge of the music. Improvisation for this type of soloing is one-sided in that there is no interaction with musicians; it is a set piece. While an expression of great skill, it lacks the deep excitement of live interaction.

The second scenario involves performing musicians: a few to several musicians in an ensemble, or an orchestra. There is a lot of variety possible in this scenario. In a later chapter in this Section, the *takht* (drum group) will be covered.

The third scenario is a hybrid, in which the dancer uses pre-recorded music, but a single drummer plays along with it. For the solo (often the end of the routine since it's difficult to start the recording again), the drummer plays alone, interacting with the dancer for a finale. For the sake of brevity, the lone drummer scenario is discussed.

Soloing to live drumming in the moment is a different experience than coming prepared with a known piece of music. Dancing

to live music requires the dancer to pay close attention to the musicians in addition to concentrating on their own dancing. It really showcases the skills of both the dancer and the musician(s). Improvisation is a continuum between chaos and manifestation, guided by the strange attractor catalyst of the mind and the moment. A drummer and dancer can, of course, rehearse ahead of time to create a set piece; the more often they work together the easier it becomes to anticipate each other, and to establish form.

There are no rules about how a solo is structured. That leaves room for a lot of variety. The drummer can play whatever he wants—tempered by the context. The dancer does not have to be stationary on the dance floor, but can move around as can the drummer. These are choices made in the moment. How, in this context, can a dancer know what to do? Experience and familiarity count, but you have to start somewhere. Observe other dancers, listen to drum solos on recordings with attention to the structure, and most importantly—practice with a drummer.

The typical length of a drum solo is around two to five minutes (or so), but can be even longer. The following is one simplistic example of a common solo structure used by many drummers for dancers:

1. A beginning section that often derives from the rhythmic pattern of the music leading into the solo, for example, *maqsum*. The drummer plays the pattern altering it by adding more and more accents (with *Dums* and *Teks*) and ornamentation. The intention is to allow dancer and drummer to establish a common ground, and for the dancer to begin to improvise using her repertoire of movements.

2. This merges into a middle section in which the tempo may accelerate, and the drummer expands upon the rhythm adding repeated figures with predictable accents. The drummer may also change the rhythm from *maqsum* to *malfuf*, for example. The middle can last as long as the dancer wishes it to. Isolation movements of the dancer's hips, torso, shoulders, head, arms, and hands are typical in this section. The drummer must be attentive to what the dancer is doing in order to reinforce these movements. Likewise, the dancer may watch the drummer's hands to anticipate accents and rhythm changes. They may play off of each other's cues—having a kind of conversation.

3. At some point, the dancer can indicate to the drummer to shift into the final section called the "shimmy." Propelled by complex, dense rolling drum patterns, it features the dancer's rapid hip motions combined with sharp hip accents synchronized to accents played by the drummer. The conclusion of the shimmy is marked by a kind of "rock 'n roll" ending (a distinct increase in the volume and rhythmic intensity of the rolls) leading to a strong *Dum* or *Tek* timed to a strong finishing gesture by the dancer.

For the drum solo scenario to work successfully, both the drummer and dancer must have knowledge of each other's art. Additionally, the dancer must be able to communicate with the musician with body expressions and motions with the eyes, mouth (and sure, speak!), arms and hands, for example. A nod or a sudden look can cue the attentive drummer. Besides using body language, the dancer must listen—the stronger the musical knowledge of the dancer, the easier it will be to resonate with the drummer. It is in the best interest of a dancer to at least learn the basics of rhythmic skills.

The drummer's knowledge of dance (both in the abstract sense and familiarity with the style) is integral to realizing a drum solo. In an interactive climate, an observant drummer is able to discern the dancer's cues and alter his patterns to match the dancer. They should be able to make her look good during the solo by reinforcing the energy with interesting ornaments, and to be able to read the direction the dancer wants to go. One of the most typical methods a drummer uses to synchronize with a dancer in a drum solo is the repetition of a phrase once or several times ending with a strongly accented riff. A typical repeating pattern ending in an accented riff is illustrated in the following example: *takita takita taka, takita takita taka, takita takita taka, Dum Dum Tek.* This is a line from the so-called *hagala* pattern known to most drummers in *danse orientale.* The use of this figurational concept is common during solos.

Performance with live drumming requires the dancer to listen intently and to move outside of herself to interact with the drummer. The same goes for a drummer; he must watch the dancer and shift beyond his own performance to synchronize with the dancer. Each must surrender a portion of ego to make a drum solo effective.

How can you learn to dance with a drummer, or drum for dancers without trying? *Just do it!* There is no reason to shy away from a live drum solo. Learn in studios with dance classes. Listen to many recordings; watch performances. There are plenty of willing drummers who could benefit from the experience—no matter what their level of expertise. When you are ready, do it in public. Don't be intimidated by what you think the audience expects. Have fun!

CHAPTER 41: DRUM SOLO SURVIVAL

So, you're out there on the dance floor, and it's time to solo with a drummer. As noted in the previous chapter "Live Drum Solos," a typical structured drum solo consists of at least three parts: 1) an intro using the last rhythm in the music prior to the solo continuing it to establish as a ground; 2) a middle section that expands on the establishing rhythm or shifts to a new one, and in which variations increase in complexity; 3) a final section—the shimmy—in which the patterns merge into a continuous stream with sharp accents placed within it for the dancer to respond to with corresponding hip and shoulder movements. What happens if none of this occurs, and the drummer is all over the place? There's no rhyme or reason to it, and there's nothing you recognize. What do you do? Where's the beat? Musicians rely on one particular skill to keep it together, and so can you. It is the *pulse*.

It doesn't matter whether the rhythm is *maqsum*, *ayyub*, or any other recognizable belly dance pattern. What does matter is the underlying *pulse* that ties it all together. It is the grid for the creation of cycles and rhythms. Listening and synchronizing to a pulse is easy. Humans are one of the primary species that perceives a regular "beat," and synchronizes to auditory pulsing with minimal conscious effort. As well, the ability to selectively hear layers of temporal structure (meter and rhythm) in music seems to be inherent in our natural abilities. Everyone has seen young children's spontaneous response to pulsed music. It's not just imitation of their elders.

Rely upon your innate sense of feeling the inner pulse underlying what the drummer is playing for you. Listen and, more

importantly, *feel* the pulse underlying the music. This is the most natural thing you can do. Move with the pulse. As your skill to hear the layers of beat improves, you will be able to sense it and have the freedom to spontaneously move. You will be grounded in the pulse, not worrying about the specific meter, rhythm, or sequence. Try to catch those accents by watching the drummer's hands for a cue to when it will happen. Trust your instincts.

CHAPTER 42: FINGER CYMBALS— ZILLING POSSIBILITIES

Zil—*zill* (Turkish), *sagat* (Arabic), *zang-e saringoshte* (Persian)— patterns can be repetitive (the same riff repeated over and over), or they can mimic or counterpoint a drum rhythm. In this article, several possibilities for zil-pattern variation are explored. As a common pattern used for belly dance, most dancers have played their zils to the 4-beat cycle dance rhythm *maqsum* (DT •T D T) or *baladi* (DD •T D T) which share the same rhythm. For the sake of expediency, only the *maqsum* rhythm is shown herein with *baladi* implied. Please note that no handing (right-left) is notated here, nor are instructions for accents, clicking, ringing, or other techniques. It is up to the zillist to choose which hand to lead with (or not), and what style and technique to use—there are many.

The following example shows the classic "gallop" pattern (zzz•) in relationship to *maqsum* (notated in its full form with *Dum, Tek,* and fill tones *tak* and *ka*; z = zill; • = silence; x = clap, the down-beat). Note also that the following notation examples below reflect a quantification of zil patterns. Live performance by a dancer is sometimes not as precise as by a musician in an ensemble or on a recording. In practice the gallop pattern, and the others shown below, are more or less synchronized to the dancer's hip side-thrusts and other motions. The gallop is often simply counted by dancers as "one, two, three," and played more freely, rather than in strict metric time and counted as "one e and •." The strict form presented here is designed to clarify the zil pattern relationship to *maqsum/baladi*.

```
x                    x                    x                    x
1    e    &    a     2    e    &    a     3    e    &    a     4    e    &    a
D    •    T    •     t    k    T    •     D    •    t    k     T    •    t    k
maqsum
z    z    z    •     z    z    z    •     z    z    z    •     z    z    z    •
classic gallop (one e and •, two e and •, three e and •, four e and •)
```

Keeping in mind the underlying 1:4 subdivision of the 4-beat cycle and the core rhythm, tap your foot on the "x" (the down-beats), or better yet, dance while playing these alternate patterns. The first set, below, is composed of repetitive patterns.

```
z    •    z    z     z    •    z    z     z    •    z    z     z    •    z    z
inverse gallop (one • and a)

z    z    •    z     z    z    •    z     z    z    •    z     z    z    •    z
loping (one e • a)

z    •    •    z     z    •    •    z     z    •    •    z     z    •    •    z
skipping (one • • a)
```

Try some of these patterns with *maqsum* or *baladi* (remember: *baladi* is the same rhythmic pattern but with different drum-tones). They can be also used for any pattern as long as you fit them to the time cycle of the drum rhythm. Try mixing them up. Play the gallop for a while, then switch to the inverse gallop and then back. Do this with the lope and the skip. This will add variety to the sound of your zilling while you dance, and it will make for a more interesting rhythm-line along with the drum patterns. Remember that the drum player is expected to vary their rhythm with fills, ornamentation, and elaboration. Why not the zilling dancer too?

Next, here are a couple of other ways of playing zils to *maqsum/baladi*. Like the repetitious patterns above, these ideas can be applied to any rhythm. The first pattern mimics the complete standard rhythm played by a drummer. This is the typical zil

pattern used by dancers when dancing to *maqsum* or *baladi*. The second pattern is a possible counterpoint of *maqsum/baladi*. Notice that the counterpoint is composed of the lope and the inverse gallop shown above. For this type of counterpoint, you can mix and match these patterns (and any others) freely— improvise!

```
x            x            x            x
D   •   T   •   t   k   T   •   D   •   t   k   T   •   t   k
maqsum
z   •   z   •   z   z   z   •   z   •   z   z   z   •   z   z
Mimic (one • and •, two e and •, three • and a, four • and a)

x            x            x            x
D   •   T   •   t   k   T   •   D   •   t   k   T   •   t   k
maqsum
z   z   •   z   z   z   •   z   z   z   z   •   z   •   z   z
Counterpoint (one e • a, two e • a, thre e and •, four • and a)
```

As can be seen, there are more zil patterns to choose from in addition to the gallop. Try some today! Listen to some zil patterns by Lily Splane at the *Zills-on-Fire* sub-site at HTTP://WWW. CYBERLEPSY.COM/DOWNLOADMUSIC.HTML. (You can download, listen, and play along with these samples to your heart's content.)

CHAPTER 43: A MUSICAL EXERCISE FOR DANCERS—RECITATION

In the same way elements of image and movement outside of so-called traditional belly dance have been combined into a fusion (Goth, Bollywood, Flamenco, Tribal, etc.), non-traditional sound materiél and it's manipulation are also sources of inspiration. The imitation of drum-tones using tuned zils is one such possibility. For an interesting group zilling experience, try using the type of interlocking technique called *hocketing* (exchange back and forth between two or more people—when one sounds the other is silent).

Hocketing was a popular polyphonic voicing style in western Europe during the 13TH and 14TH centuries. It is still an active technique in handbell choirs. The interlocking of voices and instrumental parts in different ways to create a whole melody or rhythm is found in music across central Africa stretching from coast to coast (west, middle, and east), Indonesia (Java and Bali *gamelan* music), Philippines (*kulintang* music), and the Southeast Asia (*pi phat* and *saing waing* music).

To gain a sense of the underlying time structure before playing the group piece, first try the following rhythmic skills exercises using counting and clapping. Each down-beat is subdivided into four pulses. The western relationship is one quarter-note divided into four sixteenth-notes, counted "#, ee, and, ah."

Divide the group into two sections:

1. ***Group One*** recites the counting (one, e, &, a, two, e, &, a) while clapping on the number (the down-beat marked with the X). This is the recitation of the subdivision while marking the down-beats (1 and 2).

2. *Group Two* speaks the counting (one, e, &, a, two, e, &, a) while clapping on every word. This is the recitation of the subdivisions while marking each pulse including the downbeats.

After learning this, switch around so each group has the experience of clapping and counting the down-beats and subdivision pulses. In the notation below, the symbol :|| means repeat.

1:	X				X				:||
both:	1	e	&	a	2	e	&	a	:||
2:	x	x	x	x	x	x	x	x	:||

Next, as a single group, learn to recite *ayyub* and *fellâhi* together while everyone claps the down-beats (feel the subdivisions). Clap and recite each pattern until they are memorized. Once committed to memory, recite the patterns as a single group in alternation: *ayyub, fellâhi, ayyub, fellâhi,* etc. Do not put a gap between each pattern; keep the flow, continuously cycling several iterations of the *ayyub/fellâhi* sequence. For an interesting twist, divide the group into two. While clapping together, switch the recitation back and forth between the two groups: one group speaks the *ayyub* rhythm, and the other recites the *fellâhi* rhythm.

1	e	&	a	2	e	&	a	
Dum	•	•	Tek	Dum	•	Tek	•	:||

ayyub

1	e	&	a	2	e	&	a	
Dum	Tek	•	Tek	Dum	•	Tek	•	:||

fẽllahi

Now that you have the direct experience (by clapping, counting, and reciting) of understanding the underlying time structure over which rhythmic-pattern themes called *ayyub* and *fellâhi* move, try the following fun exercises using tuned zils in the hocketing style of interlocking. Each zillist should have one pair of high-pitched zils, and one pair of low-pitched zils on each hand (it doesn't matter which hands). The smoothness of the rhythmic pattern as it is exchanged between the zillists requires a strong sense of the down-beat and the spaces (pulses) between. Keep the down-beats steady and the subdivisions clear so that the parts fit in the proper time field. In the music notation, the top line represents group one, and the bottom line group two. The symbol / denotes the bar line (the division between cycles).

In the first example, the players (*Dum* and *Tek*) maintain their parts in both the rhythms.

maintain parts

| • | • | • | Tek | • | • | Tek | •/ | • | Tek | • | Tek | • | • | Tek | • :‖ |

| Dum | • | • | • | Dum | • | • | •/ | Dum | • | • | • | Dum | • | • | • :‖ |

ayyub   *fellâhi*

In the second example, the players invert their parts (*Dum* becomes *Tek*; *Tek* becomes *Dum*) when the rhythm changes from *ayyub* to *fellâhi*.

invert rhythm and parts

| • | • | • | Tek | • | • | Tek | •/ | Dum | • | • | • | Dum | • | • | • :‖ |

| Dum | • | • | • | Dum | • | • | •/ | • | Tek | • | Tek | • | • | Tek | • :‖ |

ayyub   *fellâhi*

In the last two examples, the rhythm is maintained (ayyub or fellâhi), but the parts are exchanged every other iteration of the rhythm.

maintain féllahi invert parts

• Tek • Tek • • Tek •/ Dum • • • Dum • • •:||

Dum • • • Dum • • •/ • Tek • Tek • • Tek •:||

féllahi

maintain ayyub invert parts

• • • Tek • • Tek •/ Dum • • • Dum • • •:||

Dum • • • Dum • • •/ • • • Tek • • Tek •:||

ayyub

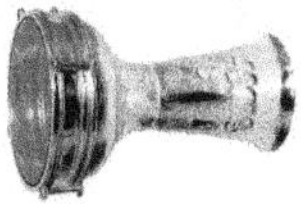

Feeling daring? Play the rhythms *ayyub* and *fellâhi* by yourself using one hand for *Dum* and the other for *Tek*. Wear low-pitched zils on the *Dum* hand, and high-pitched zils on the hand you'll play the *tek*s. Wear mismatched pairs on both hands, such as large low-pitched zils on the thumbs, and smaller, high-pitched zils on the fingers. *Experiment!*

CHAPTER 44: TRADING RHYTHMS— DIALOG BETWEEN DANCER AND DRUMMER

The better your skills at playing the zils, the more interesting your performances can become. A couple of simple variations on the standard zil pattern were suggested in the previous chapter. This chapter is a brief description of a method of interaction, a kind of dialog—trading rhythms—between the zilling dancer and the drummer in a live setting.

The borrowing of techniques and ideas from traditions outside of one's own discipline is one of the processes for refreshing the arts. Hence, the increasing emergence of so-called fusion dancing in the belly dance community with such forms as American Tribal Style and the mixing of Bollywood into belly dance, among others.

Within the last several years, in the light of dance fusion, belly dancers have begun to increasingly realize that the zils provide a musical opportunity that is woefully under-used. The Indian *sawal/jawab* (pronounced saw-WALL/ jaw-WOB) or *question/ answer* technique provides an exciting way to expand the interaction between a dancer and drummer. It is important to note that question/answer dialogs between musicians and dancers are not new to belly dance performance, but are now gaining a more visible currency. The Indian method may be considered a principle (but not the sole) inspiration for this method of interaction. A synonym for this is *call and response*—a method found in west African, Cuban, and American gospel music, for example. In Indian classical music, *sawal/jawab* has been around for a long time. It was popularized in the west by sitar master Ravi Shankar and his tabla accompanists (now deceased) Chatur Lal

and Ala Rakha (father of Ustad Zakir Hussein). His mid-60s *East Meets West* LP albums with classical violinist Yehudi Menuhin are a perfect example of this technique. Inspired by these flights of improvisational virtuosity, western fusion jazz musicians began to adopt the *sawal/jawab* in the 1970s. Among the first to do it was guitarist John McLaughlin (*Mahavishnu Orchestra*, *Shakti*, *Remember Shakti*) and keyboardist Chick Corea (*Return to Forever*). Although trading "riffs" is not a customary traditional Arabic or Turkish method, the idea is slowly finding its way into modern improvisation among contemporary players and dancers. Modern classical Persian musicians, with a historical relationship in musical theory and practice with India, have sometimes adopted this practice as well.

In classical Indian music, *sawal/jawab* is a responsorial trading of melodic and rhythmic riffs between the melodic instrumentalist (*sitar*, *sarod*, violin, *vina*, *bansuri*, etc.) or singer and the rhythm player on the tablas (North Indian Hindustani) or *mrdanga*, *ghatam*, or *kanjira* (South Indian Carnatic). This technique is also used between melody players, between drummers, or other combinations.

The general procedure in Indian music is for the melody player to begin the process during the final part of the developmental section of the piece of music. The *sawal/jawab* is set over the time cycle (measure), whatever that may be: 4-, 8-, 6-, 7-beats, and so on. For example, using a four-beat cycle, the sitarist plays a riff that lasts two cycles, and then the tabla player responds over the same number of cycles. The basic idea, as noted, is for the musicians to trade improvised riffs (sometimes it is a fixed composition). The usual way the *sawal/jawab* is realized is for the trading to proceed until a peak is reached, at which time, by tacit agreement (based on experience), the musicians enter

a closing section in the process. They reduce the number of cycles they each play back and forth until reaching unison. This reduction is called *yati goppucha*, invoking the fanciful image of the inverted triangle of the cow's tail. Much of the fun of *sawal/ jawab* is how the musicians try to trick each other or to create complicated patterns, daring the other to copy it. The following is an outline, using the 4-beat time cycle (1 2 3 4), of the structure of a common closing section used in Indian *sawal/jawab*.

? = sawal/question, A = jawab/answer

2 cycles each	? 1234 1234		A 1234 1234					
1 cycle each	? 1234		A 1234					
1/2 cycle each	? 12	A 34	? 12	A 34				
1 beat each	? 1	A 2	? 3	A 4	? 1	A 2	? 3	A 4
Unison 4 beats	1234 1234							

A simple application of the *question/answer* method is making the rounds among musicians and belly dancers in the current belly dance community. The dancer or the drummer (with the agreed upon foreknowledge that this is going to happen) initiates the rhythmic trading. What rhythms are played is up to the creativity of the dancer and the drummer. The following diagram shows a basic alternating structure in use in belly dance performance. Play during the numbers, be quiet during •.

How do you learn to do this? It does help to have had a little musical training. But, as a dancer, you should have some fundamental understanding of the time elements of the music you dance (i.e., know what a time cycle is, how to keep a beat

and subdivide it, be able to recognize and recite the fundamental rhythms of belly dance). An easy way of picking up this method is to find a piece of music in the time-cycle of four (simple is better to learn with), and practice dancing to it. It won't be the same as playing with a drummer, but it will give you experience. As illustrated above, play zils in a rhythm (make it up) for four beats, then drop out (don't play) for four beats, and then repeat the process. By doing this, you can become comfortable with alternation. If at all possible, find a drummer and practice dialog. It is important to repeat: The rhythms you play should be spontaneous, although they can be composed...but then, where's the fun in that? Be creative in your dialog!

CHAPTER 45: THE DRUM TAKHT (ENSEMBLE)

When you listen to the drumming in an Arabic or Turkish recording, what are you hearing? You may be hearing either an ensemble of drummers, programmed sound-sample sequences, one person playing all the parts (by tracking), or some combination of these methods. When you hear and see it live in person (or on audiovisual media), you have a better chance of figuring out what's going on. In modern times, sound, whether live or on a recording, is highly manipulable. In traditional live performance, multiple drum parts are performed by a *drum takht*, but tradition is changing with the times.

Background

In this article, the word *drum takht* is used, inferring an ensemble (two or more percussionists) or a section (two or more percussionists) within a band, ensemble, or orchestra. *Takht* is a Farsi (Persian) loan-word (used in Arabic and Turkish musical terminology) meaning a platform, throne, stand, or a raised bench, depending upon the context in which it is used. For example, *Takht-e Jamshid* means "Throne of the King Jamshid"— the original Persian name of the city Persepolis (renamed by the Greeks). During the Islamic Medieval and Golden Era (12TH– 15TH centuries C.E.) raised platforms were reserved for royalty, and music performers sat on a rug on the ground. The physical position (high or low) was considered a mark of the royal-peasant hierarchy established by the ancient rulers. Examples of this custom are documented in paintings and drawings from the Indian Mughal period (e.g., Akbar: 1542–1605 C.E.), and from Persian calligraphic books such as the *Shah-nameh* of Shah

Tahmasp ("Book of Kings"), with texts by Fêrdowsi (c. 1522 C.E.).

"Café culture" has provided a fertile social ground for the exchange of ideas for centuries. By the late western colonial period (c. 1850s), perhaps a European influence, most urban musicians in Beirut, Cairo, Alexandria, Tunis, Smyrna/Izmir, and Athens, etc., sat on *takhts*—raised platforms or benches (referred to as *al dekkah* or *dikkah*) in cafés. Whether sitting in a physically high position (on a stage above the audience) was an adaptation of European performance style, a deliberate comment about the relationship between the "clientele" of a café (later cabaret), a statement of defiance against old traditions, or a mix of all three, is unknown. It is probable that the Egyptian-Arab use of the term *takht* as vernacular for "band" came about through the café performance context.

At the same time, in Cairo during the late nineteenth to early twentieth century, the word *takht* came to mean a "classic" Arabic acoustic ensemble made up of 1) a vocalist, wind instrument (*nay*), 2) strings (violin [modern replacement for the traditional *kemanche*], *'ud*, and *qa'nun* [a plucked trapezoidal zither], and, 3) drum (*riq*). The *qa'nun* functions as the instrumental leader and unifier; the *riq* player is responsible for maintaining the *'iqa* (rhythmic modes). In larger *takhts*, a chorus of four to five male singers are added to reinforce the lead vocalist. Another type of ensemble, the *firqah*, which ascended in popularity over the *takht* in the 1930s, expanded the basic ensemble (by doubling the instruments, in particular the violins, and adding cello and double bass. A significant addition was the *tabla arabi*—a change from the traditional leading role of the *riq*. Big *firqah* can have as many as thirty musicians. Note that hereinafter, the term *tabla arabi* and *tabla* is used for the drum known as the *darbuka*,

dumbek, derbecki, deblek, etc.—each of the names for the drum imply acoustical differences in the shape of the drum. The term *tabla arabi* is used throughout this chapter for simplification.

After World War I, and the alteration of the boundaries and ownership of territories, western influence was in full swing. Throughout the 1930s to 1950s, the Egyptian film music industry (inspired by the West) needed big orchestral ensembles like those of Hollywood to play movie soundtracks. The classical *takht* was expanded to include a European-style string section (in other words, the *takht* morphed into a *firqah*). Other European instruments were introduced as needed. Among the instruments were the accordion and clarinet (already present in some urban bands), the saxophone and trumpet (adaptations form western symphonic brass and military music), and percussion sections using parts of the western drumset (cymbals, bass, snare, tom, woodblock, bells—all adapted themselves through other avenues of provenance). In order to sing their "hit" songs from the latest movie or 78-RPM record, film stars needed smaller groups to play nightclubs and performance halls. The large hybrid orchestras morphed into small ensembles, borrowing instruments and musical ideas from film music, and other European, American, and Hispanic sources.

Although the basic concept of a small (three to five musicians) classic Arabic acoustic ensemble remains the standard music-related definition associated with a *takht*, it is a flexible word. The meaning depends upon whether the word is used to refer to an object (platform, throne, etc.), an ensemble (band), or herein extended to mean a drum-section within an ensemble or a solo group made of only drums—the *drum takht*.

Live Performance

The instrumentation of a *drum takht* varies, depending upon the number of musicians (two or more), and the type of music (folk, classical, pop). In a two-person section, a typical combination might be a *tabla* and *riq*, a *deff* and bongos (or *naqqara*—small kettle-drums), and so on. There are many combinations possible. The following illustrates a typical percussion section found in popular Egyptian nightclub orchestras. The usual drum section consists of between two and three percussionists. The basic tonal spread—*ambitus* of the instruments—is divided between the lead (the middle- and upper-pitch ranges) and the rhythmic mode keeper (the middle- and lower-pitch ranges). A third percussionist reinforces all elements (lead and mode) in addition to providing texture.

1. The principle *tabla arabi* (treble or standard) plays the main ornamentation of the rhythmic mode (*'iqa*), directs dynamic, tempo, and mode changes, beginnings and endings, and interacts with the other players, and the dancer(s) if there are any. Note, if no second *tabla* (*sombati* or *dohola*) is available, the principle will play all parts: rhythmic, conventional ornamentations of the mode, and solos. As of 2010, there are at least five sizes of the *tabla arabi* defined by the depth of their bass-tone *Dum*, (2–5 made by the Egyptian instrument company *Gawharet El Fan*):

   - treble 14.4" x 7.5"—tenor bass
   - standard 16.9" x 8.6"—regular bass
   - *New Generation* 17.5" x 8.6"—medium bass
   - *sombati* (*sumbati, sombaty*) 18.5" x 9"—strong bass
   - *dohola* (*doholla*) 21.1" x 10.7"—extra strong bass

2. The second percussionist keeps the rhythmic mode (e.g., *maqsum*) on the *dohola*. This role is shared between the principle and second percussionists. Alternate drums played by the musician include the *deff* (a big Arabic frame-drum with jingles, 10 to 20 inches in diameter) or the *mâzhar* (a deep frame *riq*-style tambourine, 8± inches deep x 12 to 14 inches in diameter). The second percussionist sometimes plays a specialty drum during a folkloric segment of the show, e.g., *tabl al baladi* for a Sa'idi dance, or a *bendir* (a large frame-drum with a snare, 6± inches deep x 14 to 16 inches in diameter) for a Moroccan dance.

3. The *riq* (mosaic inlaid tambourine, 2.75 inches deep x 8.5 inches in diameter) is the traditional keeper of the beat, the rhythmic mode, and ornamentation, in Arabic classical music. The *tabla-dumbek-darbuka* only gained access to this role in the early 20TH century (see above). The increasing sound levels (volume) of crowded indoor café performance spaces, and other like-venues, at last necessitated a loud lead-drum (compared to the *riq*, a softer-sounding instrument) in the percussion section. The third player also doubles on various frame-drums— including the *mâzhar*, *deff*, and also like the second, the third may perform on a folkloric specialty drum such as the Sudanese tar (jingle- and/or cymbal-less frame-drum—20± inches in diameter), or the *bendir*—as needed, depending upon the music arrangement.

Notation

The following notation example is a "snapshot"—a single iteration of a cycle of four beats (a single measure in the time-cycle of four). It is one of many possible realizations and orchestrations of *maqsum* (*wazn masmudi saghir*). This example illustrates the

♩	= dum (low) [D]
♩	= tek (high) [T]
♩	= tak/ka (midtones) [t / k]
✗	= leaf cymbals
⌒	= roll

musical parts for three musicians (two *tabla arabi*—treble and bass, and one *riq*). The *dohola* plays the mode, the standard *tabla* plays the mode plus exemplar ornaments used with *maqsum*, and the *riq* plays (in this context) a light rippling fill-ornament on the disc-cymbals.

Drum Takht Orchestration

one iteration of
Maqsum
(wazn masmudi saghir)

Tabla Arabi
lead
treble drum

D   T   t k T •   D • t k T • t k

Doholla
mode keeper
baritone drum

D   T   •   T   D   T

Riq
ornamentation /
second lead
mosaic Arabic
tambourine

t • t k t • t k t k t k t • t k

© 2010 richard adrian steiger

Electronics and Hybrids

While the nightclub scene in Cairo, Beirut, Athens, and elsewhere grew, so did the use of electronic amplification and the electric guitar—an up and coming technology in the 1930s. Electronics has come a long way from the 1930s. In a recording studio, a single drummer can track all the percussion parts. The percussion and melody parts can be preprogrammed (sequenced) using computer software—live parts being added to the recording later to spice it up so it sounds more "live" and less sterile. Electronic keyboards such as the GEM "WK Oriental" are tunable to scales other than western tempered tuning, have sound samples of traditional Middle-Eastern, Indian, and African acoustic instruments, and have onboard drum machines with "ethnic" rhythm patterns. Singer-keyboardists with a *tabla arabi* accompanist are a common form of entertainment at parties and weddings. The use of a stand-alone "drum machine" (though often not operated to its potential) by a band or soloist on stage can free a solo drummer to play ornamentation without having to keep the basic *dohola* pattern (see orchestration on previous page). There are a wide variety of possible electronic and hybrid instrumentations available to a live performance percussionist. They include multi-pads, triggers, and electro-acoustic systems. Live hybrid electronic-acoustic-computer music is becoming more common. Keyboards and electronics, and drums, can be linked to computers on stage via MIDI and USB.

Conclusion

The modern definition of a *drum takht* can now include any percussion instrument, and the possibilities of being acoustic, electric, preprogrammed, or a combination of all three elements. Acoustic instruments added to the traditional *drum*

takht instrumentarium include drumset cymbals, bass drum, and, the snare drum. Latin drums such as the congas, bongo, cowbells, timbales, and West African drums such as the *jembé*, are now sometimes present. Multiple *tabla arabi* mounted in an array, popularized by the legendary drummer Raja beginning in the mid-sixties, are not now uncommon. The possibilities for the instrumentation of the modern *drum takht* are endless, limited only by the style and performance context of the music (traditional to modern). A single person may control an array of drums, triggers, sensors, and software, or any number of people can form a percussion section—and they can perform as part of a large ensemble, or as a solo act. In an evening's show, the *drum takht* may have a segment in which they step forward and play a composition.

When you listen to music on a CD, listen closely. As computer recording and mixing become the standard, all the tricks available in the digital world are being used to create music. Whether this is "fair" or not is another issue for another article. Suffice it to say, that when you watch a performance live, there may be electronics too, and it may not be easy to discern what is what. Are there human drummers, electronic devices and sound samples, loops, or a mix of all?

CHAPTER 46: THE SOURCES AND HISTORY OF RHYTHMS

Dumbek performance in Middle-Eastern music encompasses a wide scope. Conventional traditional and contextual ethnic performances (regional and emigrated) rely on established methods, and express historic cultural continuums. Extensions of tradition among ethnic Middle Easterners include the influence of western musicological elements and technology. Although practice does not always follow strict theory, three related organizational systems for rhythm, derived from classical Arabic, Turkish, and Persian theory, provide the basis for modern dumbek drumming (East and West).

Arabic

Among the initial theories of classical Arabic rhythm used in the court music of the Islamic empire, those of al-Khalil ibn Ahmad (718–786 C.E.) are considered primary. Inspired by the writings of the ancient Greeks on poetic prosody (patterns of rhythm and sound), he merged them with the regional rhythmic practices of his time into a science of Arabic prosody—the metrics and organizational structure of which provided the foundation for Arabic rhythmic theory. Al-Khalil was also influenced in part by the practices of Persia and India—and, perhaps, it may be surmised by inheritances from Neolithic, Byzantium, the Roman Empire, Central Asia, ancient Egypt, Assyria, and Babylon. Although his manuscripts (original and copied) no longer exist, he was quoted and commented upon by later theorists and musicians. Among these were the derivative works of Ishaq al-Mawsili (d. 850 C.E.), and al-Kindi (d. 870± C.E.).

The most influential of the theorists after al-Khalil is al-Farabi (d. 950 C.E.) who was a Persian. He was responsible for clarifying both theoretical and practical (performing) practices. Al-Farabi was a philosopher, a music theoretician, and a performer. As such, he was able to unify the amorphous theories on rhythm developed by al-Khalil, et al. In his first book, *Kitab al-Musiqi al-Kabir* ("The Grand Book of Music"), and then later in revisions called *Kitab al-Iqa'at* ("Book of Rhythms"), and *Kitab ihsa al-iqa'at* ("Book for the Basic Comprehension of Rhythms"), he organized rhythm into modes or *iqa'at* (singular, *iqâ*; from the verb *awqa'a*, "to let fall"). Like earlier writers, he had access to (translated) Greek writings on music. Fundamental to his rhythmic mode concept, was the idea of the Greek *Chronos Protos (tempus primus)*—a theory of time describing the smallest perceivable time point or physical percussive "attack." Al-Farabi took this point and defined three durational beats called *naqarat* (plural).

The pitches of these durations were derived from the realization of the *naqarat* on the paired bowl-drums called the *naqqara* (played with sticks). Much later in history (c. 1800s C.E.), the *dumbek* was accepted as a legitimate instrument for their realization.

1. The low-pitched "strong" beat (*naqra thaqila*) characterized as "heavy"—on the dumbek played as *Dum* (the fundamental drum-tone of the dumbek).

2. The high-pitched "soft" beat (*naqra mutawassita*) characterized as "light"—on the dumbek played as *Tak* (Arabic) or *Tek* (Turkish).

3. The mid-pitched medium beat (*naqra khafifa*) chacterized as "filling" or "ornamenting/embellishing"—on the dumbek played as *tak* and *ka* (this varies with tradition).

Each *iqa'* (rhythmic mode) was composed of sequences of *naqra*, plus a separator to designate a disjunction at the end of each cycle (realized as a rest or a durational extension). The *Iqa'at naqarat* sequences were notated with prosodic syllables (e.g., *fa'alun, ta, tan, tann*) and symbols (o, O, |). They were organized into categories based upon the dominance of the type of *naqra*: heavy, medium, or light. Al-Farabi also implied that the *iqa'at* could be thought of as measured cycles, similar in concept to the western classical musical meter. But, he also suggested that the rhythm of the prosodic lines of an *iqâ*, although cyclic in the sense of repetition, were not always fixed to meter. Rhythm can exist independently as a "free" form or within metric constraints as a "fixed" form.

The *iqa'at* by themselves were (and are) considered to be "neutral" formulas—even though each is inherently unique due to the particular arrangement of duration segments and drum-tones. To address the aesthetic aspect of performance realization, al-Farabi described at least sixteen kinds of ornamentation with attendant rules of use—an idea that is linked to the suggestions of al-Khalil ibn Ahmad. They included additions, subtractions, substitutions, contractions, and expansions. In addition to rhythmic adornment, the pulse rate (tempo), sound quality (timbre), and the use of volume range (dynamics) were integral elements to be considered. The embellishments thus functioned to bring out the sentiment and character of a rhythm. In keeping with many other musical instrument traditions, each teacher had his own "school" of method in the application of such ornaments. Ornamentation is a principle aspect of performance throughout the Middle East and Asia, and it had profound influence on early western music. These ideas, as they have developed, continue to influence modern practice.

Although somewhat unified through the Islamic Kingdom, Arabic musical practices (form, melody, and rhythm) began to diverge into separate genres beginning in the 800s—western (in Umayyadian Cordoba under Ziryab) and eastern (in Abbasidian Baghdad under Ibrahim al-Mahdi). By the 1200s, the eastern (*al-mashriq*) schools of music were in dominance. Arabic rhythmic theory during this time is considered virtually synonymous with Persian musical practice. The western regions, in semi-isolation from the eastern regions, developed a unique combination of the old classical structure in Tunisia and Algeria along with the Andalusian (*al-Andalusi*) style from Arabic southern Spain.

In Baghdad (seat of the Abbasid Kingdom), Safi al-Din al-Urmawi (d. 1294 C.E.), founded the *Systematist* school (so termed because of the organization of the notes and rhythms into modes). Safi al-Din, and his successors, further refined al-Farabi's theories and methods, enhancing al-Farabi's sometimes-fuzzy explanations. The *Systematists* also introduced a graphic notation method, which used the division of the circle as a visual device to show the structure of musical time. The circle was divided into as many segments as the number of *naqarat* syllables in a given *iqâ*. Such devices were concurrent to the development and application of geometry in art and design (as a sacred metaphor and otherwise) throughout the Islamic Empire—and have antecedents in the applications of geometry in Greece, India, and China. Linear expressions using syllables (*ta, na, nan,* etc.) in a symbolic shorthand similar to the writing out of poetic meter, like those found in the works of al-Khalil ibn Ahmad and on, continued to be used.

Numerous composite collections of flavors of *iqa'at* were generated in manuscripts using both these techniques. Safi al-Din's *Kitab al-adwar* ("Book of Cycles") included patterns of

Arabic, Persian, and Turkish origin, reflecting the extent of the international character of musical practice during that time. The rhythmic patterns in the modern Arabic *iqa'at* collective, now also known as *awazn* (plural: "measure"; singular: *wazn*), *darb* ("hit"), or *dwar* ("cycle") have encompassed all these changes, subsuming many of the historical patterns, and blending with new ones. Note that, the writing down of patterns served a different purpose at that time than modern mass-produced notation manuals. Handmade books were considered more as special objects (repository) of intellectual power (knowledge), rather than as common instruction manuals. The transmission of musical practice was direct from master to student through accretion.

Turkish

Turkish music has many similarities to that of Persian and Arabic classical court music, the connection being through the pan-Islamic unity they shared. The Turks migrated from Central Asia, arriving and integrating into the local tribes of Anatolia during the 11TH century. They brought a far-eastern flavor to their music that is distinct from that of the Arabs. After the first Turkish kingdoms of the Anatolian Seljuk period (1071–1308 C.E.), the Ottomans ascended and held power from about 1520 through 1826. The Ottomans spread their empire as far as the Maghreb (North Africa: Morocco, Tunisia, Algeria, Libya), and into Eastern Europe, assuring their influence on all these cultures. As a result of these expressions, by the early 1500s, both Arabic and Persian high-culture musical traditions declined. The relationship between the Turkish and the Armenians, Persians, Greeks, and others has been tumultuous. The "conquered" were not subsumed into the conquering culture. Both conqueror and conquered altered as a result.

The Turkish counterpart to the Arabic *iqa'at* is called the *usüller* (singular: *usül*, meaning "rule" or "code"). Similar to an *iqâ*, an *usül* is verbally expressed using a system of onomatopoeic syllables (*Dum* and *Tek*)—used to describe the sequence of tones, durations, and sequences of rhythmic patterns. *Usül* codes are taught using the recitation of the syllables, and by up and down hand gestures, and pats on the knees, reflecting the "light" and "heavy" nature of the beats. Like the *iqa'at*, *usüller* used to be performed on a variety of twin pot-drums (a.k.a., kettle-drums) called *kudüm* or *nakkare* in Turkey, and now are performed on the Turkish clay or beaten-sheet metal dumbek (a.k.a., *deblek*, *dumbelek*).

Usüller are grouped into two general kinds based upon the duration of the time cycle: small (*küçük*) and large (*büyük*). Additionally, rhythmic patterns are grouped into three categories: simple meters (2; 3; 2 + 2; 3 + 3, etc.) compound meters (2 +3; 2 + 2 + 3, etc.), and composite meters (simple and compound patterns combined into long sequences). Of the composite rhythms, the longest is known as "the beat-pattern of conquest" or *zarbi fetih*, an 88-beat rhythm comprising 80 strokes plus 8 spaces. Long patterns like this are regarded as historical, and have similar counterparts in the Arabic and Persian classical court-traditions. Like *iqa'at*, *usüller* are thought of as being neutral, and require ornamentation and variation (Turk, *vel-veleme*, meaning "clamor" or "hubbub") in order for them to manifest their character.

Another distinctive Turkish compound pattern is called the *aksak* ("limping" or "stumbling"). These rhythms are constructed of time-unit cells of two and three beats in length; for example, the ten-beat sequence called *aksak semai*, 3 + 2 + 2 + 3. The emphasis (accent) of the initial beat of each cell results in an *aksak* pattern's

characteristic asymmetrical accents. In use for dancing, *aksak* rhythms are expressed through short and long motions in space. Besides Turkey, *aksak*-like patterns are popular in the Balkans and Bulgaria.

The modern collection of Turkish *usüller* reflects the amalgam of the Turkish region (folk, urban, and classical), their historical Central Asian connections, and contacts with the cultures around them including conquests, and western classical and popular music influences. In addition to the continuance of rhythmic patterns from folk traditions and court-music, newer urban forms evolving in the 20TH century such as *Rembétika* and *Arabesk* (influenced by Arabic music) have come into existence, each with their own take on the use of rhythm. Turkish rhythms are important along with Arabic patterns in the modern rhythm repertoire.

Persian

The country of Iran is a diverse culture whose strongest ethnic component is that of the prevailing Persian culture. The historical relationship, and musical influences, of the Persian culture to those around it is vast, and cannot be addressed in depth herein. Modern Persian musicians do not use a collection of rhythms like the *iqa'at* or *usüller*, although historically they shared these traditions. Persian neo-classical compositions are arranged in suites composed of various segments like those of Arabic and Turkish art music (court music)—each with a particular rhythmic setting to fit the melodic form. Within a suite, there are free prosodic segments without a strong rhythmic pulse, segments in which there is a pulse but not a cycle, and segments that have a distinct pulse, cycle and a strong rhythmic pattern (*zarbi*, "beat" or "multiplication"; *reng*, "dance.") The segments

are assembled into various forms that ebb and flow between strong and free pulse, and prosodic and cyclic rhythm. They function like modules that can be added or subtracted from the whole as so desired by the performer. In this way, Persian neo-classical music is similar to jazz.

Persian cyclic rhythm tends to be dominated by those based on patterns of either two or six beats. The most common rhythm is the compound duple-meter six-eight—divided into two groups: 3 + 3 (6). It is characterized by accents on beats one, three, four, and five. This rhythm is sometimes referred to as *shir-e madar* ("milk of the mother"; *shir* is also translated as "lion"), referring to its importance to the cultural historic identity (*gharb-zadegi*) of Persian music. This pattern is sometimes phrased so that it works out to be a twelve-beat system, 6 + 6, with question-answer phraseology creating a quality referred to as *kereshmeh* (translated variously as "flirting," "nodding," or "lilting"). The term *kereshmeh* also refers to the classical prosodic rhythm 3 + 3 + 2 + 2 + 2.

In modern popular dance music such as that found in Los Angeles, the rhythm (and style of music) is called *shisht-hasht* ("six-eight"), and combines western and Persian elements. In current Persian neo-classical musical practice (the extension of the classical tradition), some artists (e.g., Hossein Alizadeh) use renovations of rare ancient patterns like those from the old classical Arabic and Turkish rhythmic modes. Other rhythmic patterns found in neo-classical music are drawn from Iranian folk music (e.g., Baluchi, Gilaki, and Lori-Bhaktian) using various sequences of twos and threes. For example, 2 + 3 (5); 2 + 2 + 3 or 3 + 2 + 2 (7); and 2 +3 + 2 + 3 + 3 (13). Kurdish music is an important component of the musical repertoire of Iran, and is performed by groups such as the *Kamkars,* and by neo-classical

ensembles such as *Dastan*. The dominant Kurdish time-cycles are two and seven.

Until around 1965, Iranians knew *bandari* ("from the port" or "of the harbor") only as a folk music played by oil tanker and refinery workers, harbor stevedores, and other laborers, along the coast of Iran (Persian Gulf). *Bandari* music is a syncretic mixture of Iranian (Farsi language used for the lyrics; melodies based upon Persian *dastgah*), Arabic (the *'oud* or Persian *barbat*, and a mosaic wood Arabic-style *tabla* called the *tempo arabi*), and African (two-against-three cross-rhythm and call-and-response singing) influences. The *bandari* rhythm, played in compound duple six-eight time, reflects African cross-rhythmic qualities, feeling as if it is in two-four time and six-eight time simultaneously. *Bandari* is a pan-Gulf music found in a variety of places including the southern cities of al-Basra and Umm Qasr in Iraq, in Kuwait and the U.A.E. on the Arabian Peninsula, and farther down the coast of Africa in Kenya and Zanzibar. Each region has its own flavor and names for the music. Iranians sometimes refer to *bandari* as *khâlîji* (Gulf) music, not to be confused with Saudi Arabian *khâlîji*.

In addition to the *barbat* (*'oud*) and the *tempo arabi*, other instruments used for Iranian folk *bandari* include a local bagpipe called the *ney anbân*, and the *dammâm* (with counterparts to the *tabl al-baladi*, *tupan*, and other two-sided bass drums played with stick and hands throughout the Middle East). Folk percussion includes found-instruments such as empty gas cans, oil barrels, and crates. A contemporary urban form of *bandari*, fused with western Rock, has evolved in electric dance bands. The *ney anbân* is imitated on the electric keyboard, and the old style wood *tempo arabi* is replaced by the new cast aluminum Arabic *tabla*. In the old style, a *tombak* (classical Persian wood

drum) and a *tempo* are strapped together—the drummer playing the rhythm across the two instruments. In the so-called west-coast L.A. style (U.S.A.), the drummer plays two conga drums (*quinto* and *tumba*) along with an Arabic *tabla* mounted on a stand. Keyboard players sometimes use onboard drum machines that are programmed with "ethnic" rhythms.

Persian/Iranian rhythm (in particular *shish-hasht*) is becoming known in the repertoire used by modern dumbek players, but still remains a small segment. The principle technique borrowed by dumbek players from Persian *tombak* drumming is the finger snap (*palang*). Finger snapping is also present in Turkish and Greek drumming. The snap is not easy to do on the round-edged Arabic *tabla*—it is difficult to position the hand since the drumhead is rounded and inset more from the edge compared to straight-edged type drums. Hence, drummers using the Arabic *tabla* may employ the technique, but it is not common. The technique does work well, however, on the Turkish/Syrian-type dumbek with its straight bearing-edge.

Conclusion

Over time, several regions of musical style have concentrated in Turkey, Persia, Iraq, Syria, Lebanon, Egypt, the Arabian Peninsula, and in the Mahgreb. The drumming rhythms and techniques (stick and hand) that developed in these regions have filtered into modern dumbek playing. Modern practice is a culmination of ancient and classical era theories and practices. Western influence has served as a catalyst for the reinterpretation of many of these practices. Folk, urban, academic, and contemporary expressions of music now exist side by side. The dumbek has found a niche in the contemporary western musician's instrumentarium—that is, in the percussion collections of so-called multi-percussionists,

and as a sound in the composer's palette. Innovations combining African, Western, Asian, and Latin rhythms have become *de rigueur* in current fusion music, but the traditions remain valid and viable.

Belly Dance Rhythm Resource

SECTION VI
REVIEW &
SUMMARY

The World of Belly-Dance Music
(shaded areas represent countries of origin or influence)

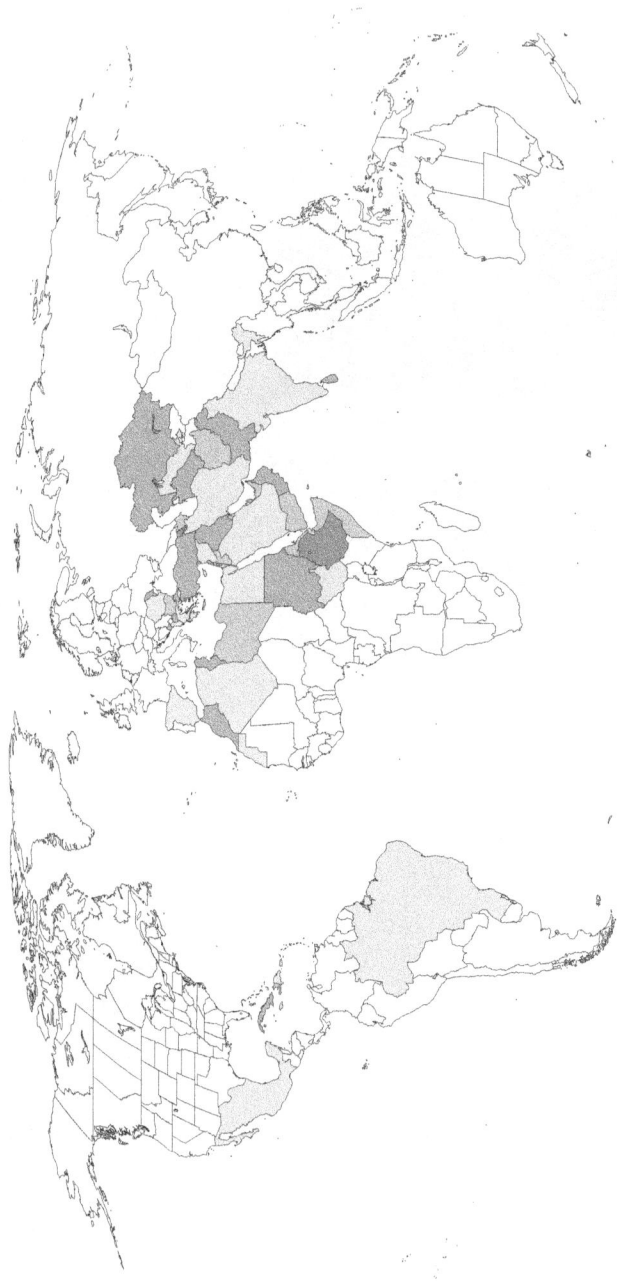

CHAPTER 47: REVIEW AND SUMMARY

Theory and History

The practitioners of classical music maintain the traditional roles in instrumentation, technique, theory, and other elements. The so-called authenticity of performance is founded upon passed-down knowledge from master to student, and through studying the writings of the scholars. Music is also learned less formally by apprenticeship and through imitation. Theory defines the parameters of a musical system, and it provides continuity over the centuries. Although practice does not always follow theory, it does provide a basis for the way music is structured. This is important for the musician *and* the dancer.

Arabic classical theory (and similarly Turkish and Persian) creates cyclic forms from small segments. These additive segments were originally arranged based upon poetic rules developed during the Golden Islamic Age. The oeuvres of classical rhythms that have come down to modern day musicians also have incorporated patterns from folk traditions and "foreign" sources that have other perceptual approaches to time theory. In most cases, the *One* is still the important beat defining the alpha/omega point of the cycle.

The history of the rhythms used in belly dance, the instruments, and all other aspects of music, not only informs the performer (dancer and musician) of their use and style, but also guides the advancement and change of such elements. The theoretical roots of the rhythms used today include influences of language (especially poetry) and math (geometry and arithmetic). Over time, several regions of musical style have concentrated in Turkey,

Persia, Iraq, Syria, Lebanon, Egypt, the Arabian Peninsula, and in the Maghreb. The drumming rhythms and techniques (stick and hand) that developed in these regions have filtered into modern dumbek playing. Modern practice is a culmination of ancient and classical era theories and practices. Western influence has served as a catalyst for the reinterpretation of many of these practices. Folk, urban, scholarly, and contemporary expressions of music now exist side by side.

The blending of culture and geography over time is a never-ending process. The interactions between the so-called Western and Eastern worlds have produced many hybrids, synergies, and even clashes of music and dance. In the realm of belly dance (*danse orientale*) as it is practiced in modern times in urban environments, the rhythms are increasingly melding. The advent of computer sequencing and remixing software coupled with performance technology has altered the way sound and performance may be delivered to an audience. Due to the use of sequencing, in particular with loops (a repeating segment of sound), a certain level of sameness occurs since there is no human producing the sound but rather a pre-recorded segment repeating. The multitude of layering and effects processing tends to obscure this lack of variety by sheer complexity. Despite this graying-out of subtle variety by mechanization, the old rhythms, instruments, and ways of performance persist and coexist with new ways.

Music Basics

Rhythm patterns are framed within a repeating cyclic system. Clocks and calendars are examples of non-musical cyclic systems. With the exception of classical Arabic and Turkish music, most belly dance music rhythms range from time cycles

of two to sixteen—with those being divisible by two or three the most common. The second is that the core melody of the drum-tone pitches *dum* (low: D) and *tek* (high: T) is attached to the rhythm, hence the term "melodo-rhythmic." These identifiable melodo-rhythmic patterns set within a time cycle are unique signatures—for example, the melodic drum-tone pattern <u>DD</u> •T D T denotes *baladi* set in a cycle of four beats. Musicians are required by necessity to understand these concepts in order to play this kind of music. It is relevant for dancers to have this basic rhythmic skill as well—to be able to know the cycle and the melodo-rhythmic core.

There are three fundamental musical essentials relevant to a belly dancer's skill to perceive and express music. The basis of music with a "beat" is simple:

1. *Pulse*—the regular tick under "music with a beat" serves as the grid or foundation over which music is set. Pulses subdivide beats. Melodo-rhythmic patterns flow over this underlying grid. This common theory has been adopted on a world-wide level among performing urban musicians. One form or another of notation (a visual method of both storing and presenting musical information—pitch, duration, form, etc.), whether very simple to very complex is also now used. The language (oral or aural) method of teaching musical patterns in addition to the student mimicking the teacher ("the rote method") is, perhaps, the oldest technique before symbolic writing, and is still in use (often in conjunction with notation). It is valuable as a teaching method requiring no visual component (reading and recognitions of a specialized symbols).

   The primary element is the pulse unit. Pulses are the stream over which the musical event occurs. The notation system

called Time Unit Boxes (TUBs) expresses this idea with boxes, each of which are equivalent to a unit or interval of time. It is a simple grid.

1 pulse   8 pulses evenly spaced

In western notation, symbols are used to mean the same thing (intervals of time), but they are various rather than simple boxes. The following example shows the equivalent time value of two "eighth-note beats" in TUBS. Pulses are the fundamental level, beats are a higher level—a beat is made of pulses.

This next example illustrates three layers of time as notated in both TUBS and in western notation. The layering of time based upon density is common to most music.

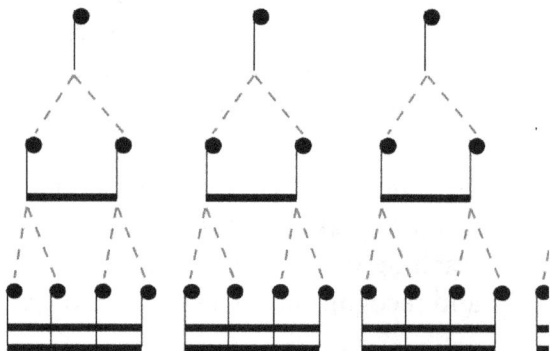

2. **Beat** and subdivisions—the *down-beat* and the *up-beat* (the down-beat is the primary beat, and the up-beat is exactly halfway between each down-beat). A repeating cycle of four beats, for example, can be counted and verbalized as "One, and, two, and, three, and, four, and..." in which the down-beats are represented by the numbers, and the up-beats by "and."

3. The **One** (the down-beat at the beginning of a cycle, for example, "ONE, two, three, four, ONE, two, three, four, and so on).

4. *Cycle*—the time-cycle or loop within which music is set can be any number of beats in length, for example, a four-beat cycle. The perception of the listener, and the intention of the performer (using specific techniques), determines the salient beat-structure of a cycle. For example, a cycle of eight beats can also be felt as four or two, depending upon how the subdivision of the down-beats and the accents are played. Cycles of beats (2, 4, 8, 7, etc.) provide the grid in which rhythms (accented and unaccented, short and long durations of sounds—like poetry) exist. To learn *any* belly dance rhythm, use the traditional method found throughout Asia and beyond—establish the time cycle by counting and clapping over and over, and then while continuing to mark the primary beats in the time cycle, recite the pattern.

5. *Rhythm*—Pulse, beat, and cycle are not rhythmic per se. It is only when pulses (called "beats" in this context) are arranged in sequences of short and long duration that *rhythm* is created. Poetic meter (think of the rhythm of a limerick) is an excellent example of short- and long-duration sounds. Belly dance rhythmic patterns are made of sequences of short- and long-pitched sounds (the high-, middle-, and low-pitched drum-tones, for example, on the

dumbek, darabukka, Egyptian *tabla,* etc.), and the empty spaces between the notes. For example, the drum-tone rhythmic sequence *baladi,* set in a four-beat cycle (counted as four beats subdivided as "One, and, Two, and, Three, and, Four, and") is Dum Dum • Tek Dum • Tek •. The word *dum* represents the low-pitched tone, and the word *tek* represents the high pitch. The dot represents a space of no sound, called a "rest" in Western terminology.

Beats are organized into repeating forms. In western theory, these groups are called *meter,* and have similar features to poetic meter. They have structures defined by points of stress and not-stress. In the case of musical meter, the principle stress is the first beat: the One. Western theory considers a cycle as a pure form (Greek influence) that can be divided into any number of segments.

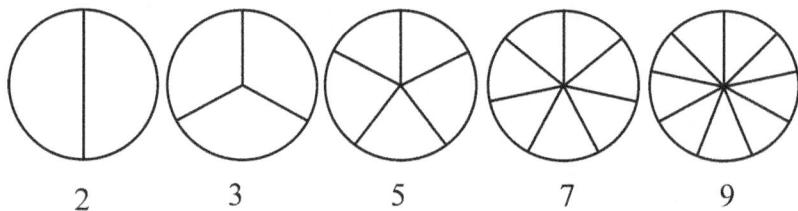

| 2 | 3 | 5 | 7 | 9 |

Cycles divided into segments

The illustration on the next page shows a cycle of eight pulses defined into a cycle of four beats. Each beat is thereby subdivided in half. One measure or cycle of this meter is counted "one, and, two, and, three, and, four, and."

eight pulses

four beats
each divided in half

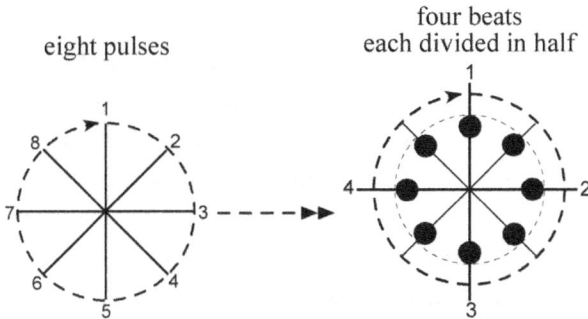

Relationship of cycles, pulses and beats

6. There are many types of *Rhythmic Modes* used for belly
dance. Each has a name and a specific rhythmic drum-tone
sequence. *Baladi* is a rhythmic mode (<u>DD</u> •T <u>D</u>• <u>T</u>•). The
examples using *baladi* demonstrate how changing the pitch
(the drum-tone) and cycle-salience, but not the rhythm,
results in several familial varieties. Rhythmic modes are
similar to melodic scale arrangements—a type of sequence.
In use, a rhythmic mode (there are numerous ones found
in "Middle-Eastern" music) is decorated (ornamented)
with ongoing rhythms played over it. They are both relative
to the mode (that is, they ornament the mode itself),
and progressive (they are in reaction to a dancer or other
musicians and are in addition to the modal decorations).
These superimposed rhythms over the rhythmic mode are
the dynamic "life" of the rhythmic performance. In most
cases (with the exception of preplanned modal decoration),
they are spontaneous to the moment. An extended
vocabulary of ornamentation is associated with each region
and locality of performance.

Music Notation

Rhythmic patterns (like all conventional belly dance rhythms) are made up of specific sequences of low- and high-pitched drum-tones (re: low-pitched *dum* and high-pitched *tek*). Three kinds of notation, for the purpose of learning, and transmission from musician to musician, are commonly used to show the relationship between a rhythm and a time cycle. They are 1) *time unit boxes* (TUBS, using a box grid with each space representing a pulse), 2) *cipher* (using letters, symbols, and/or numbers to represent pitch and time), and 3) *Western* notation (using ledger lines to denote pitch and note-symbols denoting specific time values for the rhythm. There are hybrids of these three systems. On a theoretical level, these three systems are unique graphic interpretations of sound, each with a particular useful application. It is important to note that each basic pattern represents a form of the rhythmic mode without ornamentation. Ornamentation and variation are what gives a rhythmic mode *life*.

Learning Rhythms

Many dance music CDs helpfully describe the rhythm being used for each piece. Among the many available recordings, three quality CDs demonstrating dumbek rhythms are Issam Houshan's *The Dancing Drum: Tabla Solos and Drum Rhythms*, Nourhan Sharif's *Arabic Rhythms* series, and Hossam Ramzy's *Rhythms of the Nile*. These are not "how-to" recordings; you can dance to them.

Practice your rhythms even when you aren't dancing. Sit down in a comfy chair, recline on the sofa, and clap your hands, or play your zills (with tape on the rims to prevent disturbing those near). Tap your fingers on your car's steering wheel at stop lights,

rap your fingers on your purse when waiting in line at the grocery store, play rhythms anywhere and everywhere you can. Become a walking rhythm machine….

While keeping steady time clapping your hands along with the down-beat, try to recite the rhythm's basic pattern (e.g., _dum dum • tek dum tek_). Remember, a rhythmic pattern's primary drum-tones are often deliberately _not_ on the down-beat in order to induce motion in the listener and/or dancer—they are _cross-rhythmic_ to the down-beat.

> ### Key
> • Down-beats = a number (1, 2, etc.)
> • Up-beats = the symbol &
> • Silent pulses = •
> • Claps = x

In the example below, beats in cycles of two are subdivided into four pulses shown with a double underline.

Cycles of Two

```
x                    x
1    e    &    a      2    e    &    a
D    T    •    T      D    •    T    •
```
Fêllahi

```
D    •    •    T      D    •    T    •
```
Ayyub

```
D    •    •    T      •    •    T    •
```
Malfuf

Beats in cycles of four and eight are subdivided into two pulses shown with a single underline. The cycle of nine is not subdivided.

Cycles of Four

x		x		x		x	
1	&	2	&	3	&	4	&
<u>D D</u>		•	T	<u>D</u>	•	T	•

Baladi

<u>D T</u>	•	T	<u>D</u>	•	T	•

Maqsum

<u>D T</u>	•	D	<u>D</u>	•	T	•

Sa'idi

<u>D</u> •	•	D	•	•	T	•

Khalîjî

Cycle of Eight: Chiftetelli

x		x		x		x	
1	&	2	&	3	&	4	&
D		<u>T T</u>	•	T	T		

x		x		x		x	
5	&	6	&	7	&	8	&
D		D		T		•	

Cycle of Nine: Karshlama

x	x	x	x	x	x	x	x	x
1	2	3	4	5	6	7	8	9
D	•	T	•	D	•	T	T	T

Instruments

The instruments used to play the rhythms for belly dance have deep origins, and are continuing to evolve—in name and form.

The Dumbek Family

The *dumbek's* origins, though still hazy, seem to lie outside of the Mid-East, not appearing in a recognizable form in Egypt until found in the huts of Levantine migrants after the fall of the 18TH Egyptian Dynasty. The dumbek family of "goblet" drums has four basic shapes: Cone, Hemisphere, Globe, and Cylinder.

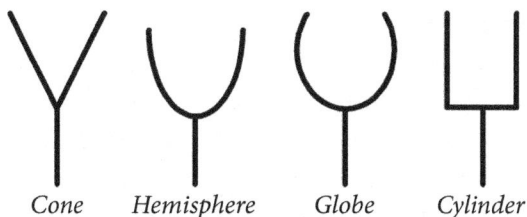

Cone   Hemisphere   Globe   Cylinder

As the instrument has developed, local culture, custom, and availability of materials determined the preferences of sound, size, shape, and material. The morphology of a given drum type effects the sound. More enclosed drums, with small waist from the resonator chamber to the tube (effusor), regenerate the drumhead's vibrations and resonate sound longer. The pitch range of the instrument is also extended, having a higher and lower ambitus than drums with wider waists. The configuration

of the ratio between the resonator chamber and the effusor tube is key to the drum type. The Persian tombak is the most resonant (small ratio), whereas the Egyptian conical drum has a wide waist and thus less sound regeneration.

The word *tabla*, among Egyptian-Arabic musicians, is used to refer to a specific conical-type clay drum—the "Egyptian," "Arabic," or "Nile" drum. The *tabla* is also known by other longer-established terms: *darabukka (derbeki, derbucca),* and *dumbek (toumbeleki, tombak).* In this book, the author has used the term *tabla arabi* for the conical Egyptian-Arabic resonator. The term *tabl* (Arabic), meaning drum, is thought to have its ancient roots in the Aramaic term *tabla,* and the Akkadian word *tabalu* or *tapalu.* T(a)bl is used as a prefix in conjunction with names of Arabic drums, such as *tabl al-baladi.* The use of the word *tabla* to refer to the Egyptian-style drum began around the late 1950s among club musicians in the Levant (*samri*) and main Arabic centers such as Cairo and Alexandria (*masri*). The term *tablas* (with an "s" added) means (to people in the North and South Indian cultures, and among the Afghani, Pakistani, and other peoples in areas connected to India) a set of two drums (treble—*tabla*; bass—*dahina*). The Indian *tablas* are specific to North India, and are considered to be derived from earlier barrel drums (cut in half to form a pair). The *tablas* are associated with classical music and rhythmic theory (*tala*), although they are used in urban and folk music as well.

Tombak

Within "Chapter 33: Shish-Hasht and Bandari" in Section IV, a brief discussion of the resonant cylindrical wooden *tombak* was given including photographs. The tombak, used in Persian music almost exclusively, represents a particular branch of the Dumbek

Family. The name *tombak* derives from the two principle tones produced on the drum: *tom* (the low tone) and *bak* (the high tone). The colloquial name for the drum is *zarb*. *Zarb* may be translated variously as "multiplication," "beat," or "rhythm." The name is used to indicate the drum itself, and "to play the beat," i.e., the *zarb*. The acoustics of the large-diameter head of the tombak, and the differential between the resonator chamber (the upper part of the drum) to the tube and the waist, allow for a rich resonance and tonal manipulation not possible on Arabic (*tabla*) and Turkish (*deblek*) dumbeks. The sound of the tombak is distinguished by the use of the resonant bass tone *tom* (similar to *dum* on the dumbek), a treble drum-tone called *kenar bak* played on the straight edge of the drum with fingertips (similar to *tek* on the dumbek) or by a left-handed snapping technique called *pâlang* (leopard). The use of complex finger-rolling ornaments is a key characteristic of tombak playing.

Certain shapes tend to be preferred in various geographical areas of the "Mid-East":

REGION	DRUM-SHAPE	COUNTRIES
Northern	Hemisphere	Turkey, continuing into Greece and the Balkans
	Globe	eastern Mediterranean islands and Greece
Middle (Levant)	Hemisphere & Cone	divided between Syria above, and Lebanon below
Southern	Cone	Egypt, Saudi Arabia
Central and Western (Maghreb)	Cone & Globe	north Algeria

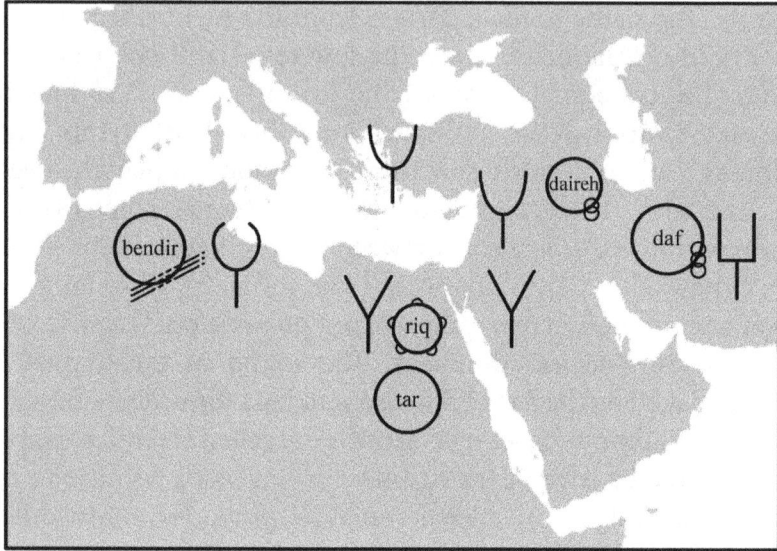

Regional drum-shape preferences

Frame Drums

Of the five frame drums discussed in "Chapter 4: Five Frames" in Section I, only one (the Egyptian-Sudanese *tar*) had no secondary sound producer. *Snares* (a line or more of a string of some kind that lays against the drum head and buzzes) are used on the *bendir* from Morocco and central North Africa. *Jingles* (small metal rings attached to the frame) are used on the *daf* (associated with the Sufis) and *daireh,* frame drums found from Turkey to Iran to the Caucasus region. The *riq* (Egypt-Lebanon) has five double-pairs of metal disks mounted in slots cut into the frame.

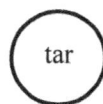

Types of Frame-Drums

Although frame drums can be used with any kind of music, they are associated with healing rituals, the roots of which are ancient. The use of secondary vibration-producing elements is considered to have its origin in trance-induction methods used by north-latitude shamans in Asia, in which the buzzing or jingling functions as a thought-distraction focusing layer in addition to the physical-mental entrainment caused by intense rhythmic repetition in the drumming itself. Both men- and women-only groups perform these rituals to drive out sickness. The rhythm (one of several that can be used) called *zar* was presented as one example (see "Chapter 24: Danse Zar—The Fascinating Rhythm," Section IV).

Rhythms

Masmudi—The "Mother Rhythm"

Many rhythmic patterns have relationships—cultural, functional, and theoretical. In music, the term *theory* means a system and method of organization (classical western music theory of triad chord harmony using tempered tuning), whereas in science, it refers to a specific aspect of a methodology which at first presents an idea to be tested, and then if accurate, represents a particular stable model (e.g., the theory of thermodynamics).

When listening to the many rhythms used for belly dance, one notices similarities. Differences in pitch, and the relationship

between the pattern and the size of the cycle (2, 4, or 8 beats), can generate a family of several interrelated modes using the same rhythmic core mode, *masmudi* (Chapter 15 in Section II).

The eight-beat cycle *wazn masmudi kabir* (big *masmudi*) is important because it is the generative model for what has been herein termed as the *Masmudi* Group—*baladi, maqsum, fellâhi,* and *sa'idi*. All these patterns derive from the Arabic classical melodo-rhythmic mode of *wazn masmudi kabir*. In Arabic theory, *masmudi* (common name), consists of two time segments (4 + 4 beats) comprising a cycle of eight beats. *Masmudi's* melodo-rhythmic core is D D • T • D • T •. In the subsequent patterns from this core, the cycle is reduced into four beats or two beats while retaining the essential pattern. Note the substitution of the second *Dum* with a *Tek* in *maqsum, sa'idi,* and *fellâhi*; and the addition of a *Dum* on the & (and) of two in *sa'idi*. The following diagram illustrates the relationship of *masmudi* to the other patterns.

Wazn masmudi kabir (8-beat cycle)

DD •T D T
Baladi (4-beat cycle)

DT •T D T
Maqsum (4-beat cycle)

DT •D D T
Sa'idi (4-beat cycle)

DT•T DT
Fêllahi (2-beat cycle)

Masmudi's relationship to other rhythm patterns

Sa'idi

Sa'idi (a traditional folk pattern from the Egyptian Sa'idi region), has become the standard Arabic pop-music rhythm. One may surmise that it is because of its similarity to a standard rock 'n roll rhythm that it has gained such popularity. The following example shows the standard rock groove, and then the traditional *sa'idi* pattern in drumset notation. TUBs is used to show the traditional pattern. The first snare back-beat of the rock pattern is offset ahead (the "and" of *One*) in the *sa'idi* pattern giving it a syncopated feel.

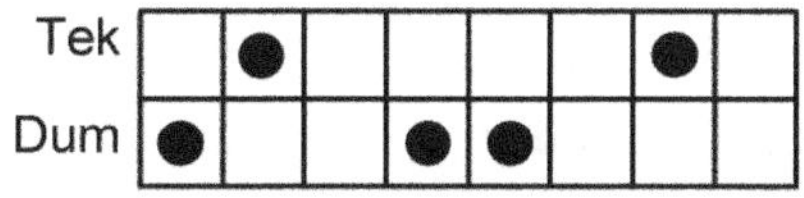

Sa'idi (4)

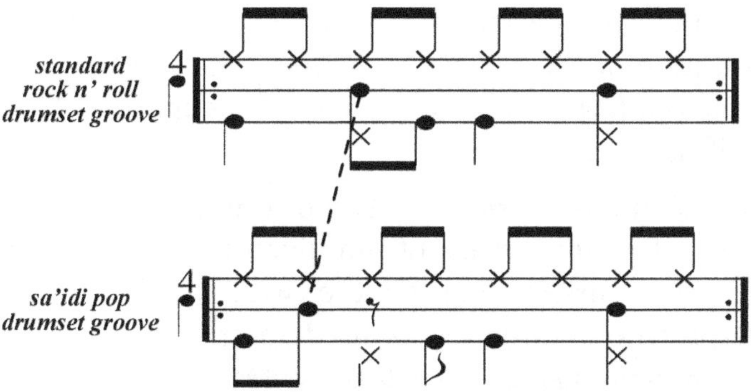

standard rock n' roll drumset groove

sa'idi pop drumset groove

Sa'idi Rhythm compared to the same rhythm played in western "pop" style

	?		A	
2 cycles each	1234	1234	1234	1234

	?	A
1 cycle each	1234	1234

	?	A	?	A
1/2 cycle each	12	34	12	34

	?	A	?	A	?	A	?	A
1 beat each	1	2	3	4	1	2	3	4

Unison 4 beats	1234 1234

Beats and Cycles

The traditions of performance of a given rhythm—that is, its place of origin, function in society, and cultural significance—are not always clear. For example, the origins of *chiftetelli* and *karachi* are obscure. They both are derivative.

Chiftetelli

It is surmised that the *chiftetelli* rhythm (and name) evolved out of an imitation of the two-pitch drones used on certain double-pipe wind (e.g., the *kaval*) and string instruments (e.g., *lyra* and *bagalama saz*). The rhythm has three general forms:

1. the northern style, inclusive of Turkish and Greek (mainland and island), Roma, and Armenian music. This category is the most diverse in structure and tempi,

2. the southern style, inclusive of Arabic music. The principle realization of the *chiftetelli* rhythm is the condensed form called *wahda e nous* ("one and a half" or *dar e nous*, "hit and a half"),

3. The fusion *danse orientale*-style of Europe and the U.S.A. merges the influences of immigrant performers from Armenia, Turkey, and Greece with modern Western interpretation. *Chiftetelli* is used in this style as a slow section in multi-part belly dance suites.

Karachi

Karachi is an adapted rhythm (by Arabs) from Latin American music. It is interesting to note that this rhythm is an example of reverse migration—its probable origin is Africa, was taken to the Americas and the Caribbean, hybridized and adapted, and then returned back to be used by musicians of Africa—specifically Arabs. (This is the same case as the Arabic, Persian, and Chinese

instruments that made their way into Western Europe, eventually becoming the orchestral instruments we know today. Many of those instruments such as the violin, keyboards, and guitar, have been absorbed back into Arabic, Persian, and Turkish music.) Although the name *karachi* suggests that it is from Pakistan (the name is the same as Pakistan's capital city Karachi), it is probably not from there. It does have some similarities to the pan-Indian *bhangra* dance rhythm *chaal*, but the overall quality of *chaal-bhangra* is quite different from *karachi*. *Bhangra* swings and has a "skippy" feel, while *karachi* is played flat without any swinging quality. Whether there is a historical relationship is questionable. The other more likely derivation of *karachi* is the *guaracha* pattern from Latin American music. The *guaracha* is similar to *karachi* in two ways. First, the two names *karachi* and *guaracha* imply a possible vowel or consonant shift due to language and pronunciation differences. Second, the low-pitched tone in *guaracha* is placed on the "and" of down-beat two like *karachi*. These two similarities suggest some possible connection. It also has similarity to Cuban *rumba* and *calypso* counter-rhythms.

Complex Rhythms

In the chapters "Five and Ten," "Karshlamá," and "Eleven" of Section III, the additive concept was discussed. Additive time-cycles and rhythms consist of cells of two (binary) and three (ternary) beats. The concept of sequencing (adding) together short (2) and long (3) cells is a common method in creating rhythmic structure. Cycles and patterns created with sequences of twos and threes may either be "even" or "odd" depending upon the number of total beats of the cycle (2, 3, 4, 5, 6, 7, 8, 9, 10, 11, 12, etc.). Several examples were given demonstrating the variety of arrangements of groups of cells. With the exception of *karshlamá*, these rhythms are not typical to belly dance, but

are potential sources of interesting dance accompaniment. These chapters explored the repetition of an "odd" meter (non-quadratic) creating a symmetrical form, making them suited for dance routine segments using call-and-response or question-answer mirrors of movement.

Karshlamá

The musical expression of the same basic pattern changes depending upon the geographic and cultural region in which it is played. Distinctions exist among northern, middle, and southern styles of playing the *karshlamá*.

The example below shows different ways of notating the nine-beat cycle Turkish-Armenian rhythm *karshlamá*. Four segments of varying length (2 + 2 + 2 + 3 = 9) are assembled to create a recurring nine-beat cycle, upon which a sequence of drum-tones (pitched drum-sounds) are repeated as a structural rhythm foundation upon which the musicians play (and dancers dance).

The pattern is shown in TUBs (with symbols representing drum-tones low and high), Western notation, and in cipher notation. Cipher notation uses letters and numbers. Here the letters of the words of the drum-tones (D= *Dum*, the low-pitched tone, and T = *Tek*, the high-pitched tone) are used

Karshlama

segments: ● 2, × 2, ● 2, ××× 3

pitched TUBs

cipher   D • T • D • T T T

Western 9/8

along with some borrowed note value notation (underlines and dots). The *chobiyya* and *jurjuna* rhythms (see "Folk-Dance Rhythms" on page 245) have additive structures.

Persian 6/8 Rhythm

Even though there are other species and varieties of rhythms in the cycle of six (Arabic, Maghrebean, Turkish), *shish-hasht* (six-eight) and *bandari* (from the harbor or port) are relevant rhythms from Iran. The Persian sixes are reflections of Persian high culture and of international blending. *Shish-hasht* (six-eight), the most commonly known six-beat rhythm of Iran, is a musical meme in the Persian culture. Its origins are thought to be in the poetry of the ancient Persian kingdoms. The rhythm is sometimes referred to as *shir-e madar* (literally, "milk of the mother")—inferring its importance to Persian cultural identity. (The word *shir* also means "lion" in Iranian Farsi.) It is identifiable by the special twist or lilt from the accents that occur on beats one, three, four, and five (the down-beat is on one and four).

The second type of rhythm, *bandari,* is not Persian, but rather Iranian, in the sense that it does not have a provenance connecting it to classical Persian culture. *Bandari* is both a musical style and a dance whose original context is found in the ports or harbors (*bandar*) along the Iranian coast in the Persian Gulf. B*andari* is a *syncretic* folk music—a mixture of Iranian, Arabic, and black African music and movement unique to the Persian Gulf—played by oil tanker and refinery workers, stevedores, and other laborers. It is sometimes referred by Iranians as a *khalîji* (Gulf) rhythm and music, but is not the same as the Arabic rhythm known to belly dancers by the same name. Other similar forms exist in the Persian Gulf along the coasts of Iraq and the eastern Saudi Peninsula, although it's not called *bandari* or sung in Farsi.

Variants are also found along the eastern coast of Africa as far down as Kenya, along the coasts of Pakistan and India, and wherever Iranian sailors traveled. Like many other "folk" music, modern recording technology and media have altered the way *bandari* is experienced and used. With the influx of western Rock 'n Roll into Iran in the 1960s (the Beatles and Rolling Stones, etc.), urban musicians in bandar-e Abâdan and bandar-e Abbâs, for example, began to adapt folk music to the electric band. By the mid-1990s, *bandari* had become an established feature in Persian dance clubs in Los Angeles and elsewhere.

Bandari has a strong "three against two" feel since the accents are placed both every other beat as well as every third beat. The diagram below illustrates this. *Bandari* is usually phrased so that the first six beats are the "call" and the second three beats are the "answer." This is effected by beginning with lower-pitched drum-tones in the first set of six, and higher-pitched drum-tones in the second set of six. Note the letters "t" and "q" represent the conga drums *tumba* and *quinto* used in addition to the dumbek in the modern "L.A."-style bandari created by Iranians who immigrated from the war-torn city of Abadan in the Persian Gulf.

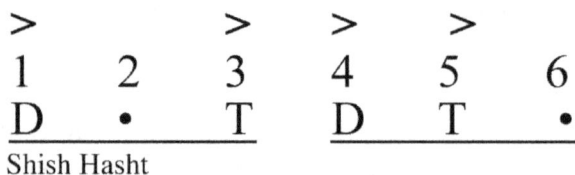

>		>	>	>	
1	2	3	4	5	6
D	•	T	D	T	•

Shish Hasht

Persian 6/8—"Shish-Hasht"

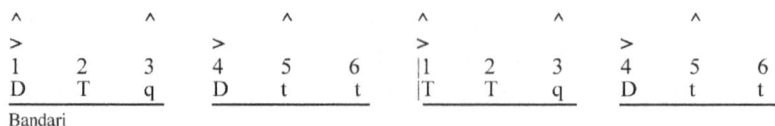

^		^	^			^	>	^	^		
>			>			>			>		
1	2	3	4	5	6	1	2	3	4	5	6
D	T	q	D	t	t	T	T	q	D	t	t

Bandari

Iranian Bandari Rhythm

Seven (7/8 Rhythm)

"Chapter 20: Flavors of Seven" in Section III analyzed how rearranging the order of groups of two (2) and three (3) beats, making up a seven-beat cycle, can be permutated (2 + 2 +3; 2 + 3 + 2; 3 + 2 + 2) to create new rhythms. Reordering manifests different "flavors."

Folk-Dance Rhythms: Debke, Chobiyyah, & Jurjuna

We explored three folk-dance rhythms used for group line-dancing: the *debke* (Lebanon), *jurjurna* (Armenia), and *chobiyyah* (central Iraq). Line dancing occurs widely throughout the Eurasian continent. Although these particular rhythms are found in popular entertainment and art music, they have a primary role within their respective communities (in native and immigrant contexts). The rhythms function as unifying and celebratory processes at weddings and other communal or private social gatherings.

In addition to the linear dance aspect, these dances (*debke*, *jurjuna*, *chobiyyah*) are characterized by complex steps, and by an accent or "heavy" step (stomp) used to emphasize the beginning, middle, or end of the sequence in the repetition of the rhythmic cycle. Complex is meant as foot crossing, doubling, and shifting with successive repetitions of the cycle. Beginner steps are simple; more experienced dancers progress to more complex steps. Since these dances are culturally embedded, children learn them early through imitation and association. It is outsiders that have the most difficulty, unless they have studied folk dance. Each participant holding the shoulder, waist, or hand of the next forms the line. It is headed by a man (typically, but women fulfill this role as well) holding (twirling) a handkerchief, *masbha* (prayer beads), or other objects such as chains. The line

may move and weave across the dance floor or remain stationary. The line may become a circle at times, but is not considered to be a "circle dance" by dance ethnologists. Participants break in and out of the line, and the leader may change during the course of the dance, which may last several songs. The line, shape of the movement, the object the leader holds, the rhythm, and the manner of stepping are all imbued with significance to the community. Each locality has its own variant flavor and meaning.

On a musical level, these folk-dance rhythms, like the *masmudi* group, *shish-hasht*, and *bandari*, are set in a time cycle, and have recognizable melodo-rhythmic patterns. The sequence of the low-pitched *Dum* and the high-pitched *Tek* drum-tones make the pattern clear, and guide the dancers. *Debke* and *chobiyyah* are characterized by multiple *Dums*, and *jurjuna* by its accented mirror grouping of beats (3 + 2 + 2 + 3). *Debke* has a "grounded" quality to it, emphasized by the *tek* on beat four. *Chobiyyah* and *jurjuna* have a "rolling" quality, creating a sense of propulsion. The following are basic examples of *debke* (4), *chobiyyah* (4), and *jurjuna* (10):

1	&	2	&	3	&	4	&
D	D	T	D	D	•	T	•

Debke

1	&	2	&	3 e & a	4 e & a
D	D	D	T	D • • T	• • T •

Chobiyyah

Iraqi *chobiyyah* has an interesting dual characteristic. It is analyzable as a kind of extension of the *malfuf* rhythm. *Chobiyyah* (like *debke*), has several rhythms that can be used for the dance, and this is only one example.

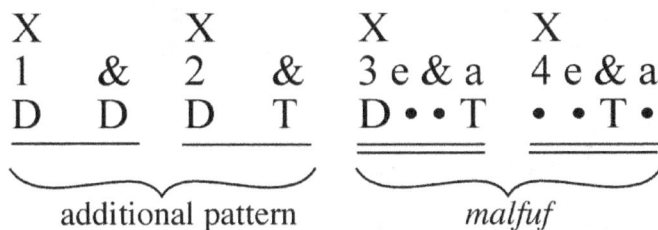

X		X		X	X
1	&	2	&	3 e & a	4 e & a
D	D	D	T	D • • T	• • T •

additional pattern   *malfuf*

"Dual-Character" of Chobiyyah

1	2	3	4	5	6	7	8	9
D	•	•	T	•	D	•	T	•

Jurjuna

Jurjuna, a ten-beat cycle rhythm, is claimed by Armenians, Iraqis, Turks, and others. Its true origin is unknown. This rhythm is traditionally played on frame drums, as are the *debke* and *chobiyyah*. Jurjuna's structure is made of four segments: 3 + 2 + 2 + 3 = 10. Compare this to the example of the nine-beat cycle rhythm *karshlamá*.

Boléro

The *boléro* rhythm (see "Chapter 32: Danse Orientale Boléro," in Section IV) probably came from Algeria to Spain, passed from the French composer Maurice Ravel (March 7, 1875–December 28, 1937) to Cuba, and has traveled back again. What the basic

Algerian rhythm was, is unknown. The first westernized *bolèro* is reputed to have been created by Sebastian Cerezo in Cadiz, Spain, around 1780. It is purported that he heard this pattern while visiting Algeria. Cerezo's initial form of the *boléro* was set in a time cycle of three beats. The examples below show Ravel's "classical" *Boléro* (first written as a technical etude before it became popular), and a cipher-notation example of the *danse orientale* or Arabic *boléro*. The shift from a three- to a four-beat cycle to set the rhythm likely comes from its further adaptation for different dance types (Spanish vs. Arabic).

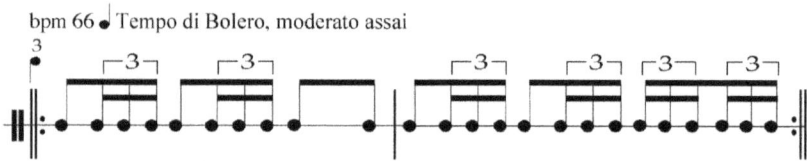

Maurice Ravel's "Bolero"

1	&	2	&	3	&	4	&
D	tkt	T	k	T	k	D	k

Arabic Boléro

Arabic or "Danse Orientale" Bolero Rhythm

Zar and Ayyub

"Chapter 24: Danse Zar—The Fascinating Rhythm," in Section IV briefly touched upon how the so-called standard *zar* pattern, adapted into belly dance routines from the healing and trance-inducing ritual of the same name, is really *ayyub* slowed way down.

The "Hidden" Pattern

Another bit of analysis was discussed concerning the so-called "hidden" pattern made up of 3 + 3 + 2 beats. It is an accented arrangement of durations that scan, like poetic prosody, into a sequence of long, long, short. This 3 3 2 sequence is explicit in three belly dance rhythms (*pop-khalîji*, *ayyub*, and *malfuf*), and is prevalent in Hispanic music.

Rhythmic Ambivalence

A more discerning discussion on the effect of uncertainty in whether the salient down-beat feels binary (two) or ternary (three), was analyzed in "Chapter 35: Rhythmic Ambivalence," in Section V. Groups of three and two, making cycles of six- or twelve-beats provide a context for this effect. A six-beat cycle can be grouped as 2 + 2 + 2 or 3 + 3. A twelve-beat cycle expands the possible combinations. For example, twelve can be grouped as 4 + 4 + 4, 6 + 6, or a hybrid like 2 + 2 + 2 + 3 + 3 (6 +6). The combination of playing three over two creates an interesting rhythmic ambivalence. The effect of the shift of beat-salience between three and two provides a dynamic possibility for dance.

Cross-Rhythm

Another rhythmic mode central to a family group incorporates cells grouped by accent into a sequence of 3 + 3 + 2 = 8. This 3 3 2 sequence is found in Latin, African, Middle-Eastern, and other musical cultures. Part of this is due to migrations and the mixing of cultures. In "Chapter 14: Malfuf," in Section II and "Chapter 27: Khalîji," in Section IV, various aspects of the 3 3 2 mode were explored. The relationship of the "odd" 3 3 2 rhythm to the "even" time-cycle creates a syncopation effect. This topic was detailed in "Chapter 36: Cross-Rhythm," in Section V.

Drum Solos, Zils, Call & Response, Hocketing

The fundamentals of beat, cycle, and rhythm were applied in "Chapter 40: Live Drum Solos" and "Chapter 41: Drum Solo Survival," both in Section V. Although there is a typical structure (one of several that can be shown), underneath all the rhythmic activity is the pulse (beat) unifying the dancer and the drummer.

In "Chapter 42: Zilling Possibilities," also in Section V, I advocated that simple zil pattern variation, and the copying of rhythms (using *maqsum* as an example), are starting points for the dancer to create a lively relationship with other dancers and with musicians. Along these lines, "Chapter 44: Trading Rhythms—Dialog Between Dancer and Drummer" illustrated a question-answer form adapted from north- and south-Indian music. It was popularized by sitarist Ravi Shankar and his tabla player Alla Rahka (father of Zakir Hussain), and adapted into jazz by guitarist John McLaughlin and keyboardist Chick Corea, for example. The chapter presented how a group of dancing zillists could be divided into two groups (**?**: question, and **A**: answer) to create a musical conversation. A reductive pattern (in this example), the group **A** musicians play rhythms for two cycles, then group **B** musicians respond by playing an answering pattern for two cycles. As the musicians continue, they reduce the number of cycles and beats until they are playing in unison. The dancer (zils) and drummer can musically converse with this sort of structure or can play free-form. Being strong in the basics of rhythm also allows for the synchronization of group zil performances. In "Chapter 43: A Musical Exercise for Dancers— Recitation," one such example using tuned zils was presented. The interlocking of two zil parts by means of the technique called *hocketing*, was employed to mimic the dumbek's pitches, *Dum* (low) and *Tek* (high). The rhythms *ayyub* and *fellâhi* were used as a source for these exercises.

Drum Takht

During the late 19TH to early 20TH century in Cairo, the word *takht* referred to an ensemble made up of a vocalist and a number of instrumentalists. The "set" of instruments from this ensemble type came to represent a kind of standard. The instruments included winds, strings, and drums. The original lead drum was the *riq*. The exchange of the quieter *riq* (small tambourine) with the louder *tabla arabi* as the lead drum in urban ensembles and popular music is an example of change caused by the electrification of music. As popular Arabic ensembles flourished in the 19TH and 20TH centuries, and as they were adapted to nightclubs and to provide the music for belly dancers, the role of drumming shifted from support only, to also soloing like a melody instrument. The "drum solo" section of a dance routine gave rise to an expansion of percussive instrumentation. The one or two percussionists of the traditional classical *takht* ensemble were increased with more percussionists. The term "drum *takht*" is used to refer to this larger group of percussionists. Acoustic instruments added to the traditional *drum takht* instrumentarium now can include drumset cymbals, bass drum, and the snare drum. Latin drums such as the congas, bongo, cowbells, timbales, and West African drums such as the *jembé* (also spelled *djembé*), are sometimes present. There are sets of *tabla arabi* ranging from small to large size (like the span of the violin family: violin, viola, cello, and bass). Multiple *tabla arabi* mounted in an array, popularized by the legendary drummer Raja beginning in the mid-sixties, are not uncommon today. With the advent of digital technology, a *drum takht* includes any percussion instrument. It includes the possibilities of being acoustic, electric, pre-programmed, or a combination of all three elements.

Belly Dance Routines

Belly dance shows are based on *routines*—a music "program." Arabic and Turkish belly dance routines are set in a suite form. In other words, there are several parts (three to seven) strung together, each piece with a different rhythm. A typical medium-length suite for belly dance:

1. begins with a fast entry section (e.g., *ayyub, malfuf,* or *fellâhi*),

2. that merges into the first medium-tempo piece (e.g., *baladi* or *maqsum*).

3. The music slows down into a sensuous piece (e.g. *chiftetelli, masmudi,* or *boléro*) in which the dancer does a veil dance or "floor work."

4. At the conclusion, music becomes faster, and the drummer stands out and begins the drum solo (freestyle).

5. When complete, the music then shifts into an up-tempo piece or two (back to *baladi* or *sa'idi,* or even *karshlamá*) in which the dancer "works" the room.

6. The suite may end with a repeat of the entry music (e.g., *ayyub* or *fellâhi*), except that it is instead, for exiting.

These parts can be assembled, and added to or subtracted from, in any way the dancer and musicians agree. The recognition of the rhythms is critical to how the dancer moves. Each rhythm has its own characteristic and emotion for the dancer to express. *Baladi* is not *sa'idi*—the dance moves for each are different; zils are played differently.

The chapter "Chapter 39: A Classic Belly Dance Routine—Raks Mustapha," addressed the overall form of a "typical" belly dance routine. It analyzed how various rhythms were played in

a deliberate sequence that reinforced the type of dance being performed. The form also created a dramatic arc for the dancer to follow.

In Conclusion

It is hoped that the material covered in this book will advance the dancer's understanding of rhythm, and the foundations of the patterns that are used in belly dance. Listen to live performances and apply your rhythmic skills. Make it a goal to learn the basic rhythms. You don't have to be a drummer to learn them by recitation and clapping—this is a fundamental skill. Indeed, if you are a dancer, learn to *play* the drum. It will improve your dancing and zilling immeasurably. Hold semi-monthly group get-togethers in your house, a large backyard, or a park, and *teach each other* drumming.

About
Richard Adrian Steiger

I began learning how to play the *dumbek,* and accompanying belly dancers on it, on the Gypsy Stage at the San Marcos Renaissance Faire in 1988 as a paid performer for the "play gypsy" band (with Steve and Ana Ball, and Philip Marcus). It was great fun, and a new instrument and type of music to learn. Having already been involved in other musical traditions for many years (Indonesian gamelan; Indian classical; and Persian classical, folk, and pop), I was eager to absorb another. Little did I know that I would still be involved. I've grown to love belly dance, the music, and its culture.

Early on, as a trained ethnomusicologist (M.A., SDSU 1988), I realized that there was little written work on the rhythmic material used for belly dance. My scholarly interests couldn't be quieted. I began writing an instructional book (since I couldn't find one I liked) on how to play the dumbek. It soon turned into what I called "bookzilla." The name came about because the project became far more than an instruction manual. It includes chapters on the drum's history, the cultural context, physics, and other elements. In other words, it became a big scholarly project. It is still not finished (life has a way of diverting one's attention), and it is my intention for 2015 to complete the book and get it out there. As part of the process of researching and writing, the idea of doing informational articles about the rhythms for dancers for *The Papyrus,* the SAMEDA (San Diego Area Middle-Eastern Dance Association) newsletter, became attractive (a place where I could work out ideas, and hone my writing skills). At the request of several SAMEDA staff members, I started submitting a few occasional articles on my research. In 2007, I was asked to start a monthly column on music (now totaling 72 consecutive articles).

For access to their publication as a monthly column writer, I am profoundly grateful to SAMEDA. Thank you for the voice.

I have met and performed with many excellent dancers from whom it has been an honor to learn about this dance, and from musicians from whom I learned the minutia of dance accompaniment. To all of you whom I have met along the way—*thank you!* I hope my articles have been useful.

From those articles, this book was born—the articles edited, compiled, merged, and converted to chapters, now all in one place, arranged in manner that hopefully engages and benefits dancers of all levels. Thank you, Lily Splane for all your hard work. I didn't even think about making my article collection a book.

Contact:

RICHARDASTEIGER@YAHOO.COM

Visit:

HTTP://WWW.CYBERLEPSY.COM/DUMBEK.HTML

REFERENCES

Acoustics

Campell, Murray, and Clive Greated. *The Musician's Guide to Acoustics*. New York: Schirmer Books, 1987.

Leitner, Alfred. "Vibration of a Circular Membrane." *The American Journal of Physics*. 35.11 (November 1967): 1029–1031.

Moravcsik, Michael J. *Musical Sound: An Introduction to the Physics of Music*. New York: Solomon Press—Paragon House Publishers, 1987.

Balkan

"Traditional music: Bulgarian dance rhythms." *Eliznik webpages*. Liz Mellish and Nik Green. HTTP://WWW.ELIZNIK.ORG.UK/BULGARIA/MUSIC/ (last mod. 6 April 2006).

Bhangra

Kalsi, Johnny. "Dhol notation [for Bhangra]." Dhol Foundation. HTTP://WWW.RHYTHMZONE.CO.UK/DHOLNOTATION.PDF (accessed 12 June 2014).

Bolèro

Gradante, William and Deane Groot. "Rumba." In *The New Grove Dictionary of Music and Musicians*, ed. Stanley Sadie and John Tyrrell, 4: 329. London: Macmillan, 2001.

Orenstein, Arbie. *A Ravel Reader: Correspondence, Articles, Interviews*. Minneola, NY: Dover Publications, 2003.

Steinberg, Michael. "Ravel Boléro." *Program notes for San Francisco Symphony.*
http://www.sfsymphony.org/Watch-Listen-Learn/Read-Program-Notes/Program-Notes/RAVEL-Bolero.aspx (accessed 19 September 2014).

Stigberg, David. "Spanish Boléro." In *The New Harvard Dictionary of Music*, ed., Don Michael Randel. Cambridge, Massachusetts: Harvard University Press Reference Library. The Belknap Press of Harvard University Press, 1986.

Culture

Pacholcyzk, Jozef M. "Secular Classical Music in the Arabic Near East." In *Musics of Many Cultures*, ed. Elizabeth May, 253–268. Berkeley: University of California Press, 1980.

Racy, 'Ali Jihad. "Music in the 19TH century Egypt, a Historical sketch." *Selected Reports in Ethnomusicology* 4 (1983): 157–179. Los Angeles: U.C.L.A. Publications.

———. "Sound as Society: The Takht Music of Early Twentieth Century Cairo." *Selected Reports in Ethnomusicology* 7 (1988): 139–170. Los Angeles: U.C.L.A. Publications.

Debke

Chabrier, Jean-Claude, "Music in the Fertile Crescent: Lebanon, Syria, Iraq." *Cultures: Music in a Changing World.* Unesco: La Baconnière.1.22 (1974): 35–58.

Greek Rhythms and Dance

Holden, Rickey, and Mary Vouras. *Greek Folk Dances.* Newark, New Jersey: Folkraft Press, 1965.

Indian Theory

Brown, Robert E. *The Mrdanga: A Study of Drumming in South India.* 2 volumes. Ann Arbor: University Microfilms, 1965. PhD dissertation. U.C.L.A.

Stewart, Rebecca Marie. *The Tabla in Perspective.* Ann Arbor: University Microfilms, 1974. PhD dissertation. U.C.L.A.

Wade, Bonnie C. *Music In India: The Classical Traditions.* Englewood Cliffs, New Jersey: Prentice-Hall, 1979.

Instruments

"Arab Tahkt." *Qatar Music Academy.* HTTP://WWW. QATARMUSICACADEMY.COM.QA/EXPLORE-AND-LEARN/ LEARN/ARABIC-MUSIC (accessed 9 June 2014).

Anoyanakis, Fivos. *Greek Popular Musical Instruments.* Athens: National Bank of Athens, 1979.

Boddy, Janice. *Wombs and Alien Spirits: Women, Men, and the Zar Cult in Northern Sudan.* Madison: The University of Wisconsin Press, 1989.

Buonaventura, Wendy. *Belly Dancing: The Secret of the Sphinx.* London: Virago Press Limited, 1983.

Brindle, Reginald Smith. *Contemporary Percussion.* New York: Oxford University Press, 1970, revised edition, 1991.

Buchner, Alexander. *Folk Music Instruments of the World.* New York: Crown Publishers, 1972.

Carlton, Donna. *Looking for Little Egypt.* Bloomington, Illinois: IDD Books, 1994.

Collaer, Paul, and Jürgen Elsner, et al. *Nordafrika Musikgeschichte in Bildern* [Music History in Pictures]. Band I: Musikethnologie/Lieferung 8. Leipzig: VEB Deutscher Verlag für Musik, 1983.

Daniel, Francisco Salvador, ca. 1830–1871. *The music and musical instruments of the Arab: with introduction on how to appreciate Arab music edited with notes, memoir, bibliography and thirty examples and illustrations by Henry George Farmer.* Portland, ME.: Longwood Press, 1976.

el-Dabh, Halim. *The Derabucca: Hand Techniques in the Art of Drumming.* Publication, no. 6993. New York: Edition Peters, 1965.

Hassan, Scherazade Qassim. *Les Instuments de Musique en Irak, et le rôle dans la societé traditionnelle* [The Instruments of Music in Iraq, and their role in traditional society]. Paris: Editions de l'école des hautes études en Sciences Sociales, 1975.

Hickmann, Hans. "La Daraboukkah." *Bulletin de l'Institut d' Egypte, Cairo.* 33 (session 1950–1951): 229–245.

Hoest, Georg. *Nachrichten von Marokos und Fes, im Lande selbst gesammlet, in den Jahren 1760–1768* [News from Maroko and Fez, gesammlet in the country itself, in the years 1760–1768]. Copenhagen: Christian Gottlob Prost, 1781.

Jenkins, Jean, and Poul Rovsing Olsen. *Music and Musical Instruments in the World of Islam.* London: World of Islam Festival Publishing Co. Ltd., 1976.

Kakish, Wael. "Al-Takht." *Nashrat Kan Zaman: Classical and Folkloric Arabic Music.* Kan Zaman Community Ensemble. HTTP://WWW.KANZAMAN.ORG/ (accessed 2 March 2010).

Nieuwkerk, Karen van. *A Trade Like Any Other: Female Singers and Dancers in Egypt.* Austin: University of Texas Press, 1995

Picken, Laurence E.G. *Folk Musical Instruments of Turkey.* London: Oxford University Press, 1975.

Redmond, Layne. *When the Drummers Were Women: A Spiritual History of Rhythm.* New York: Three Rivers Press, 1997.

Touma, Habib. *The Music of the Arabs.* New expanded edition. Trans. Laurie Schwartz. Portland, Oregon: Amadeus Press, 1996. s.v. "Wazn."

Jurjuna

"Armenian dance." In *Wikipedia, The Free Encyclopedia.* Wikimedia Foundation, Inc. HTTP://EN.WIKIPEDIA.ORG/ WIKI/ARMENIAN DANCE (accessed 31 August 2014).

Laz

"Laz." *Middle Eastern Rhythms FAQ.* HTTP://WWW.KHAFIF.COM/ RHY/ (accessed 22 November 2014).

Tastekin, Fahim. "Turkey's Laz Awakening." *Al-Monitor: The pulse of the Middle East.* HTTP://WWW.AL-MONITOR. COM/PULSE/ORIGINALS/2013/12/LAZ-PEOPLE-OF- TURKEY-AWAKEN.HTML# (last mod. 1 December 2013).

Nine (9/8)

Lamb, Evelyn. "Uncommon Time: What Makes Dave Brubeck's Unorthodox Jazz Stylings So Appealing?" *Scientific American Online.* December 11, 2012. HTTP://WWW. SCIENTIFICAMERICAN.COM/ARTICLE/UNCOMMON-TIME- DAVE-BRUBECK.

Rhythm Analysis

Cooper, Grosvenor, and Leonard P. Meyer. *The Rhythmic Structure of Music.* Chicago: University of Chicago Press, 1960.

Creston, Paul. *Rational Metric Notation. The Mathematical Basis of Meters, Symbols, and Note Values.* Hicksville, New York: Exposition Press, 1979.

Manuel, Peter. "The Anticipated Bass in Cuban Popular Music." *Latin American Music Review / Revista de Música Latinoamericana* 6.2 (Autumn–Winter, 1985): 249–261.

Patel, Aniruddh D., John R. Iversen, Yanqing Chen, and Bruno H. Repp. "The influence of metricality and modality on synchronization with a beat." Experimental Brain Research. Springer-Verlag Link. 163.2: 226–38. HTTP://WWW.HASKINS.YALE.EDU/REPRINTS/HL1387.PDF (accessed 11 November 2014)

Toussaint, Godfried. "The Euclidean Algorithm Generates Traditional Musical Rhythms." *Proceedings of BRIDGES: Mathematical Connections in Art, Music and Science,* Banff, Alberta, Canada, July 31-August 3, 2005. Extended version. HTTP://CGM.CS.MCGILL.CA/~GODFRIED/PUBLICATIONS/BANFF-EXTENDED.PDF (last mod. 11 December 2006).

Persian Music

Nasehpour, Peyman. "A Research for the Different Names of the Tonbak (Persian goblet drum)." *Peyman and his Tonbak.* Peyman Nasehpour. HTTP://TONBAK.WORDPRESS.COM/2007/04/03/ZARB-OR-TONBAK-PERSIAN-DOUMBEK/ (accessed 3 February 2014).

Nettl, Bruno. "Persian Popular Music in 1969." *Ethnomusicology.* Journal of the Society for Ethnomusicology (SEM) 16.2 (1972): 218–49.

Tehrani, Ostad Hosein. *Amouzesh-e Tonbak* [Rudiments of the Tombak]. Tehran, Iran: Ministry of Culture and Arts Printing House, 1350/1972.

Zonis, Ella. *Classical Persian Music: An Introduction.*
Cambridge: Harvard University Press, 1973.

Rhythmic Theory

"Arabic rhythms: Muwashahat." *Maqam World.* Maqam World.
HTTP://WWW.MAQAMWORLD.COM/RHYTHMS.HTML (last
mod. 14 July 2007).
"Traditional Arabic Music: Music structure: wazn." *Classical
Arabic Music.* Multi Media Publishing. HTTP://WWW.
CLASSICALARABICMUSIC.COM/MUSIC%20STRUCTURE.
HTML. (last mod. 11 November 2013).
Racy, 'Ali Jihad. "Sound as Society: The Takht Music of
Early Twentieth Century Cairo." *Selected Reports in
Ethnomusicology* 7 (1988): 139–170.
Sawa, George D. "Theories of Rhythm and Meter in the
Medieval Middle East." In *The Garland Encyclopedia
of World Music*, ed. Virginia Danielson, Scott Marcus,
and Dwight Reynolds, 6: 387–93. New York: Routledge,
2002.
"World Music and Ethnomusicology—Two Views." *College
Music Society Newsletter.* UCLA Herb Alpert School of
Music. Dale A. Olsen, Florida State University.
"World Music and Ethnomusicology—Understanding the
Differences." Robert E. Brown, San Diego State
University.
"World Music—Past, Present, and Future." HTTP://WWW.
ETHNOMUSIC.UCLA.EDU/WORLD-MUSIC-AND-
ETHNOMUSICOLOGY. (last mod. May, 1992).

Routine: Ya Mustapha

"Bob Azzam" In *Wikipedia, The Free Encyclopedia*. Wikimedia Foundation, Inc. HTTP://EN.WIKIPEDIA.ORG/WIKI/BOB_AZZAM (accessed 29 April 2014).

Meissoun. "Ya Mustapha! A Song Conquers the World." *Gilded Serpent*. HTTP://WWW.GILDEDSERPENT.COM/ART32/MESSIOUNMUSTAFA.HTM (accessed 6 May 2012).

"Ya Mustafah" In *Wikipedia, The Free Encyclopedia*. Wikimedia Foundation, Inc. HTTP://EN.WIKIPEDIA.ORG/WIKI/YA_MUSTAFA (accessed 17 November 2014).

Seven (7/8)

"Kalimatianos." *Wikipedia, The Free Encyclopedia*. Wikimedia Foundation, Inc. HTTP://EN.WIKIPEDIA.ORG/WIKI/KALAMATIANOS (accessed 11 November 2014).

"Septuple meter." *Wikipedia, The Free Encyclopedia*. Wikimedia Foundation, Inc. HTTP://EN.WIKIPEDIA.ORG/WIKI/SEPTUPLE_METER (accessed 21 October 2014).

Turkish Rhythm

"Turkish usûller." *The Oud*. David Parfitt. http://www.oud.eclipse.co.uk/usuller.html (last mod. 16 October 2014).

Holzapfel, Andre and Yannis Stylianou. "Rhythmic Similarity in Traditional Turkish Music." *Proceedings of 10TH International Society for Information Retrieval Conference* (ISMIR 2009): 99–104.

Zar

Bizzari, Heba Fatteen. "The Zar Ceremony." *TourEgypt.net*. HTTP://WWW.TOUREGYPT.NET/FEATURESTORIES/ZAR.HTM (accessed 6 June 2014).

Fakhouri, Hani. "Zar Cult in an Egyptian Village."
    Anthropological Quarterly 41.1 (1968): 49–56.
Harding, Karol (Me'ira). "The Zar Revisited." *Crescent Moon
    Magazine*, July–Aug 1996, 9–10.
"Rania Khallaf sways to esoteric rhythms." *Al-Ahram Weekly
    Online.* Al-Ahram Weekly, Cairo. 9–15 November 2006,
    no. 819. HTTP://WEEKLY.AHRAM.ORG.EG/2006/819/FE2.
    HTM (accessed 6 January 2010).

IMAGE SOURCES

All photographs and graphics by R.A. Steiger, except:

Page 11
The Wilkinson "Darabooka," a fellahîn-style drum
"Darabooka" (tabla arabi and tombak), circa 1859. Original
source from Edward William Lane, *An Account of the Manners
and Customs of the Modern Egyptians.* 2 vols. 3RD edition.
London: Charles Knight and Co., circa 1856. "Darabukkeh,"
2.2: 87, 88. Reused by Sir John Gardner Wilkinson in *A
Popular Account of the Ancient Egyptians.* 2 volumes, revised
and abridged. New York: The Bradley Company Publishers,
1878. Illustrations by Joseph Bonomi from drawings by author
and others [Lane]. "Darabooka" 1: 98–99. Image source used:
"Derbekkeh, Palestine," picture p. 580 in W. M. Thomson:
*The Land and the Book; or Biblical Illustrations Drawn from
the Manners and Customs, the Scenes and Scenery of the Holy
Land.* Vol. II. New York, 1859. HTTP://COMMONS.WIKIMEDIA.
ORG/WIKI/FILE:DERBEKKEH, P. 580 IN THOMSON, 1859.JPG
(accessed 7 May 2014). Wikicommons.

Page 13
Khatam tombak, Ibid.

Page 14

Globe drum 1, Globe drum 2
"Darbuka." Morocco, 1955. Tropen Museum accession nr.
2439–34. Web: HTTP://COMMONS.WIKIMEDIA.ORG/WIKI/
FILE:COLLECTIE_TROPENMUSEUM_ENKELVELLIGE_
BEKERTROM_VAN_AARDEWERK_TMNR_2439-34.JPG .
Wikicommons.
"Darbuka," Nabeul, Tunisia, 1912. Staatliche Museen zu
Berlin (State Museum Berlin, SMB), Preußischer Kulturbesitz,
Ethnologisches Museum: Nordafrika, West- und Zentralasien.
SMB ID: III B 2415. Barbara Pischel collection. Photographed
by Susanna Schulz for SMB. Web: HTTP://WWW.SMB-DIGITAL.
DE/EMUSEUMPLUS?SERVICE=EXTERNALINTERFACE&MODULE
=COLLECTION&OBJECTID=196047&VIEWTYPE=DETAILVIEW
Wikicommons.

Page 15

Vase-type globe drum
"Darbuka." Morocco, 1955. Tropen Museum accession nr.
3492–3. Web: HTTP://COMMONS.WIKIMEDIA.ORG/WIKI/
FILE:COLLECTIE_TROPENMUSEUM_ENKELVELLIGE_
BEKERTROM_VAN_AARDEWERK_TMNR_3492-3.JPG.
Wikicommons.

Page 19
Photo: Lily Splane (Richard playing dumbek for a live
performance)

Page 20
Photo: F. Bahrami

Page 21
Photo: unknown guest at wedding reception

ART EXAMPLE SOURCES

Page 16 (text only)

Bida, Alexandre F. (1813–1895). "The Tabla Player," (FR: Joueuse de Tarabouqa—The Tarabouqa Player). *Souvenirs d'Egypte* [Souvenirs of Egyt]. Paris: Impr. Lemercier, 1851. BW engraving. New York Public Library Digital Collections (beta). NYPL catalog ID (B-number): b13982628. UUID: 0b57f950-c6bc-012f-068a-58d385a7bc34. HTTP:// DIGITALCOLLECTIONS.NYPL.ORG/ITEMS/510D47D9-682C-A3D9- E040-E00A18064A99 (accessed 2 August 2014).

Page 16 (text only)

"Woman Playing a Drum." (n.a.) *Victoria and Albert Museum*, London: England. Oil on calico. Image ID: 712-1876. Tombak, Qajar Period (1787–1925). HTTP://COLLECTIONS.VAM.AC.UK/ ITEM/O133577/WOMAN-PLAYING-A-DRUM-OIL-PAINTING- UNKNOWN/ (accessed 12 December 2015). Image example: HTTP://WWW.BBC.CO.UK/ARTS/YOURPAINTINGS/PAINTINGS/ WOMAN-PLAYING-A-DRUM-30255 (accessed 23 November 2014).

SELECTED PERSONAL COMMUNICATIONS

Arab World

- Morwenna and Walid Assaf (Lebanese debke) [2012]
- Issam Houshan (Syrian rhythms and technique) [2005]
- Ali J. Racy, Ph.D (classical Arabic rhythm lecture/demo) [1994]
- Richard Bahram (belly dance drumming, rhythms, classic cabaret performance) [1988]

Armenia

- John Bilezikjian (jurjuna)
- Var Daghdivarian (jurjuna)

Iraq

- Louay Yousif, musical director, 2012. St. Peter Chaldean Catholic Church, El Cajon, CA. (Iraqi /Arabic rhythms)

Kurdish

- Jani Diylan (Kurdish rhythms)
- Çiwan Haço (Kurdish rhythms)

India

- Robert (Bob) E. Brown, Ph.D (classical Indian rhythm theory and history, *tala dasa prana* [Sanskrit: 10 life-breaths of rhythm])
- Kishore Banerjee (tablas, rhythmic skills and theory)
- Trichy Sankaran (mrdangam, kanjira, rhythmic skills and theory)

Iran

- Amir-Abbas Etemadzadeh (tombak, daf technique, rhythms, theory)
- Pejman Hadadi (tombak, daf technique, rhythms, theory)
- Mohammad Reza Lotfi, master class (tombak technique, rhythms, theory)
- Hossein Omoumi. Lecture: "Description of the systems in

Persian classical music, the role and importance of poetry, and common traits between Persian music and architecture," at The NeuroSciences Institute, San Diego, CA, February 9, 2003. (rhythm theory, history, instrument building)

- Ali Sadr (tombak, daf, zur kane technique, rhythms, theory)
- Mahmood Shamshiri (tombak, Bandari)

Latin World

- Michael Spiro (tresillo, rhythm theory, rhythms, technique)

Turkish

- Latif Bolat (Sufi rhythms)

www.ingramcontent.com/pod-product-compliance
Lightning Source LLC
Chambersburg PA
CBHW031243090426
42742CB00007B/291